Montana and the West Series
IV

LIEUTENANT COLONEL GEORGE A. CUSTER

The Custer Mystery

by
Charles G. du Bois

Upton & Sons   2000
El Segundo, California

Copyright 1986
Charles G. du Bois

All rights reserved including the rights to
translate or reproduce this work or parts
thereof in any form or by any media.

LIBRARY OF CONGRESS CATALOG CARD NUMBER 86-50291
ISBN 0-912783-06-0

Second printing, 2000

Contents

Foreword by Lawrence A. Frost 9
Preface 15
1 "Setting the Stage" 19
2 "Where the Sister Saved Her Brother" . . . 33
3 "The March up the Rosebud" 41
4 "Reconnaissance in Force" 55
5 "The Valley Fight" 71
6 "The Battle on the Bluffs" 81
7 "The Mystery" 97
Epilogue 129
Roster 139
Bibliography 169
Notes 171
Index 187

Illustrations and Maps

Lt. Col. George A. Custer . . . . . . *frontispiece*
PORTRAITS . . . . following page 17
  Maj. Marcus A. Reno
  Capt. Edward S. Godfrey
  Capt. Thomas Custer
  Capt. Frederick W. Benteen
  Capt. Myles Keogh
  Crow King
  Curly-Crow Scout
  Rain-in-the Face
  Sitting Bull
  Two Moon
  Gall
MAPS
  Movement of the Three Columns, 1876 . . . 18
  Rosebud Creek/Little Big Horn region 35
  Route of the troops at the Battlefield 96
  Indian Encampments 96

All photographs are reproduced courtesy of the
Custer Battlefield National Monument

FOREWORD
by Lawrence A. Frost

I was first introduced to Charles du Bois at Superintendent Major Edward S. Luce's residence at the Custer Battlefield National Monument in 1948 and became captivated by his account of using a World War II mine detector at the Medicine Tail ford, Deep Coulee and Deep Ravine. At that time he was Program Director for radio station KBMY, Billings, Montana.

On July 17, 1950, he recorded for radio broadcast the ground breaking ceremony for the present Custer Battlefield Museum. Major Luce was master of ceremonies, Colonel Brice W.W. Custer, General Custer's grandnephew, turned over the first spade of earth and I made some remarks in behalf of the Custer family in Monroe and the Monroe County Historical Society of which I was president.

In 1959, Charles du Bois was ordained into the Episcopal Church. Later he became the rector of St. Andrews Episcopal Church in Rapid City, South Dakota, remaining there until his retirement in 1984.

Many historians consider the battle of the Little Big Horn an event of little significance as far as history is concerned. This may be true. Yet it, like Pearl Harbor, awakened this nation to a growing threat to its western expansion and development. In each instance insurmountable problems had developed between contending cultures to such a degree war appeared to be the only solution.

The battle of the Little Big Horn was a battle of decision, an engagement that would determine who would control the country west of the Missouri River.

George Armstrong Custer was the one selected to spearhead the 1876 expedition to drive the recalcitrant Indians back onto their reservations. The Indians had violated their rights by encroaching on land belonging to other tribes. When he departed with General Alfred Terry's letter of instructions he, unknowingly, had two strikes on him.

In making what Custer authority Dr. Charles Kuhlman referred to as a "reconnaissance in force" Custer was unaware that:

a) Indian agents had falsified their census counts by failing to indicate that a great number of Indians were off their reservation.

b) General Crook, while leading 1,300 cavalrymen against those Indians off their reservations, had been soundly defeated by 1,500 Cheyenne and Sioux warriors on the Rosebud River a week earlier and had made no effort to inform Custer of his calamity.

When Custer charged the Indian village thinking he had reliable information as to the number of Indians there and adequate support he was unaware that Major Reno would fail to obey his orders to charge it. And he did not suspect that Captain Benteen would refuse to obey orders to bring up the reserve ammunition that was with the pack train. Thus, his two immediate subordinates provided the third strike.

Greed impelled the Indian agents to act as they did. To decide what motives lay behind the deliberate vacillation and procrastination of Custer's subalterns is a bit more difficult to determine.

Custer's defeat was a remarkable consequence. As an extraordinary field commander, a master technician — his previous successes are proof enough — as Lieutenant Colonel

Morris, in his article "Custer Made A Wise Decision," said of Custer, his was a "well-armed, well-led, well-organized, professional unity of 225 men... and did what his superiors expected him to do."

Why did the Indians fight so well? Was it inspiration and exultation as the result of defeating Crook or was it desperation resulting from the pressure of white expansion and occupation of their hunting grounds?

Their leaders realized their way of life was being challenged by forces larger and better equipped than theirs. When joined by the forces that defeated Crook the tribes assembled in the Little Big Horn valley were exhilarated by news of their great victory.

When Reno attacked them in the valley they met him fearlessly as was their custom when protecting their families. Reno's ignominious retreat added to their self-confidence. There was no thought of capitulation, no evidence of desperation.

The Indians had been in the habit of covering the retreat of their families fleeing from their villages when attacked by a hostile force. In this instance they had no time to escape. They did what they were forced to do — fight off the Seventh Cavalry's surprise attack. Custer did what he had to do when confronted by hostile adversaries — attack before they escaped. His greatest concern was the likelihood they might escape.

In Custer's book *My Life on the Plains* and in my *Court-Martial of General George Armstrong Custer* there is ample evidence that he studied and understood the habits, psychology and guerrilla warfare techniques of the Plains Indians. Lieutenant Colonel Robert E. Morris (Instructor in Military and World History at West Point) in his "Custer Made a Good Decision" (*Journal of the West,* July 1977) observed that:

1) "Indians will not attack and close with large bodies of troops.

2) "It is practically impossible to catch hostile villages in the summer.

3) "If a village is attacked winter or summer, Indians will fight only to escape."

Crook and Reno outdid themselves in displaying their incapacity by their inaction, irresponsibility and disobedience. The Indians recognized and responded to those signs and won signal victories. As a result, their self-respect and self-confidence was restored.

Both General Nelson A. Miles and General Jesse M. Lee, who was the recorder for the Reno Court of Inquiry, were of the opinion that Major Reno's disastrous retreat resulted in keeping out of the battle at a critical period fully three-fifths of the effective force, and in doing this all chance for victory over the Indians was lost. Custer's plan did not fail. It was the failure of officers in which he placed his trust to carry it out.

As Morris said, "Custer was one of the best field commanders West Point ever produced." But no one can be perfect.

The Custer battle was in an election year, at a time in which elected officials strain to present their best side. The Republican administration made every effort to sever any resemblance of association with the calamity. What better opportunity to place the blame. Custer was a national figure totally unable to defend himself. Though this was a ruthless political diversion it served their purpose to label him a "grandstander." Today he probably would be labeled a "hotdog."

Not long after the Civil War he had faced a barrage of verbal and printed abuse to which he responded by saying he had no reason to fear real bullets nor had he any of paper bullets.

Two years later (1867) he had been the target of nervous Washington politicians seeking relief from public criticism because of General W.S. Hancock's disastrous campaign against the Plains Indians. Following it Custer became the

FOREWORD   13

recipient of a court-martial. The original charges were of little consequence but those tacked on resulted in the court finding him guilty for which he was sentenced to a year's leave of absence without command or pay proper. Ordinarily he would have been given a reprimand for having made a questionable move. Congressional leaders, disturbed by the public reaction to excessive military expenditures and to Hancock's unsuccessful campaign against Indians, found it expedient to make Custer the scapegoat. Apparently it was part of a political plan to divert public criticism.

Addressing the subject by using a different approach du Bois provides a broad background for the events that culminated in a major military disaster and a political setback to an irresponsible Washington administration. Understandable accounts have been few. This is one a reader can comprehend. There have been numerous written accounts and interpretations of the battle and countless unwritten ones. Some are scholarly and some are logical. Many are realistic. du Bois' account is both scholarly and realistic. There are few men living who have devoted as many years as he has to an in-depth and on-the-field study of the Custer battle. Yet he makes no pretense of offering a final answer. However he does present his interpretation and opinion of what happened to Custer and his five companies of the Seventh Cavalry.

Facts and unprejudiced conclusions are presented in a manner that is readable, plausible and logical. Here, perhaps for the first time, a background is provided that uncovers much of the mystery. With this one can understand why two cultures clashed and why the foremost field commander this country had produced was destroyed while making what many military authorities claim was a good decision.

Lawrence A. Frost
Monroe, Michigan

PREFACE

Everyone loves a mystery, a fact that perhaps explains the proliferation of books and articles produced over the past century to tell the story of the Battle of the Little Big Horn. Compared to Waterloo and Gettysburg, Little Big Horn does seem insignificant, yet it continues to confront us with what is surely one of the most enigmatic puzzles in military history.

This book does not pretend to present the final answer to this puzzle, but merely to propose my own interpretation of the evidence, and offer one more opinion of how the five companies of the 7th Cavalry Regiment under the command of Brevet Major General George Armstrong Custer met death on the heights above the Little Big Horn on June 25, 1876. The story, of course, cannot be taken out of context; it must include the events surrounding it, all of which contribute in some way to the making of the Mystery.

Wherever possible, I have tried to tell the story in the words of those who lived it, both Indian and white, for they are the only sources we have. In these quotations it will be noted that the officers under the command of Generals Terry and Crook are addressed by their contemporaries according to their brevet ranks — temporary grades awarded them for their Civil War exploits. Custer and Gibbon, for example, were Major Generals during the Civil War, but in the shrunken table of organization of the peacetime army, they were reduced to lieutenant-colonel and colonel, respectively. Except in official documents, both were always addressed as "General," and the same may be said for others of lesser brevet rank. Marcus Reno, the junior major of the 7th Cavalry, and Frederick Benteen, the senior captain, were addressed by their brevet rank: colonel. Some of the regiment's other officers, while serving as captains and lieutenants, held brevets of lieutenant colonel and captain. There is nothing dishonest in distinguishing these men by the ranks they held in the Civil War; common military courtesy demanded it then, and it seems appropriate to continue this practice today.

The major tributary of the Bighorn River is more properly called the "Little Bighorn," according to present day usage. However, it was once called the "Little Horn" by some and the "Little Big Horn" by others. I have adopted this latter form here, chiefly as a salute to my fellow members of the organization which also uses this form in its title: "The Little Big Horn Associates," and hope that they will accept it as a "symbol of sodality."

I am indebted to Richard G. "Dutch" Hardorff of DeKalb, Illinois, for his generosity in sharing with me information not otherwise available, and I would be remiss if I failed to recommend his excellent book, *Markers, Evidence and Indian Testimony,* as a first-rate alternative to my own theory.

I will always be grateful to the late Major Edward S. Luce, a former "Garry Owen," and former Superintendent of the Custer Battlefield, and to his wife Evelyn, for their help and encouragement in the late 1940's until their retirement in 1956. It was during those years that my long-standing friendship with Dr. Lawrence A. Frost began, and his many contributions to the Custer Story have earned him a well deserved place of honor in the hearts of his many friends and colleagues. His, and the Luce's encouragement, resulted in my first attempt to tell the story: *Kick the Dead Lion* in 1954.

In 1951, my wife, Lee, told a friend that she "lost her husband at the Battle of the Little Big Horn," a statement that can be made by a number of wives whose husbands have been bitten by "the Custer Bug," but as far as I know, she said it first! When I think of all the weekend treks to the Battlefield she endured, I realize that her contribution — her patience and understanding — is the one for which I am most grateful. Though it is of small recompense, Lee, this is for you!

CHARLES G. DU BOIS
Rapid City, South Dakota

Major Marcus Albert Reno

Captain Edward Settle Godfrey

CAPTAIN THOMAS CUSTER

CAPTAIN FREDERICK W. BENTEEN

CAPTAIN MYLES KEOGH

CROW KING

CURLY-CROW SCOUT

RAIN-IN-THE-FACE

SITTING BULL

Two Moon

Gall

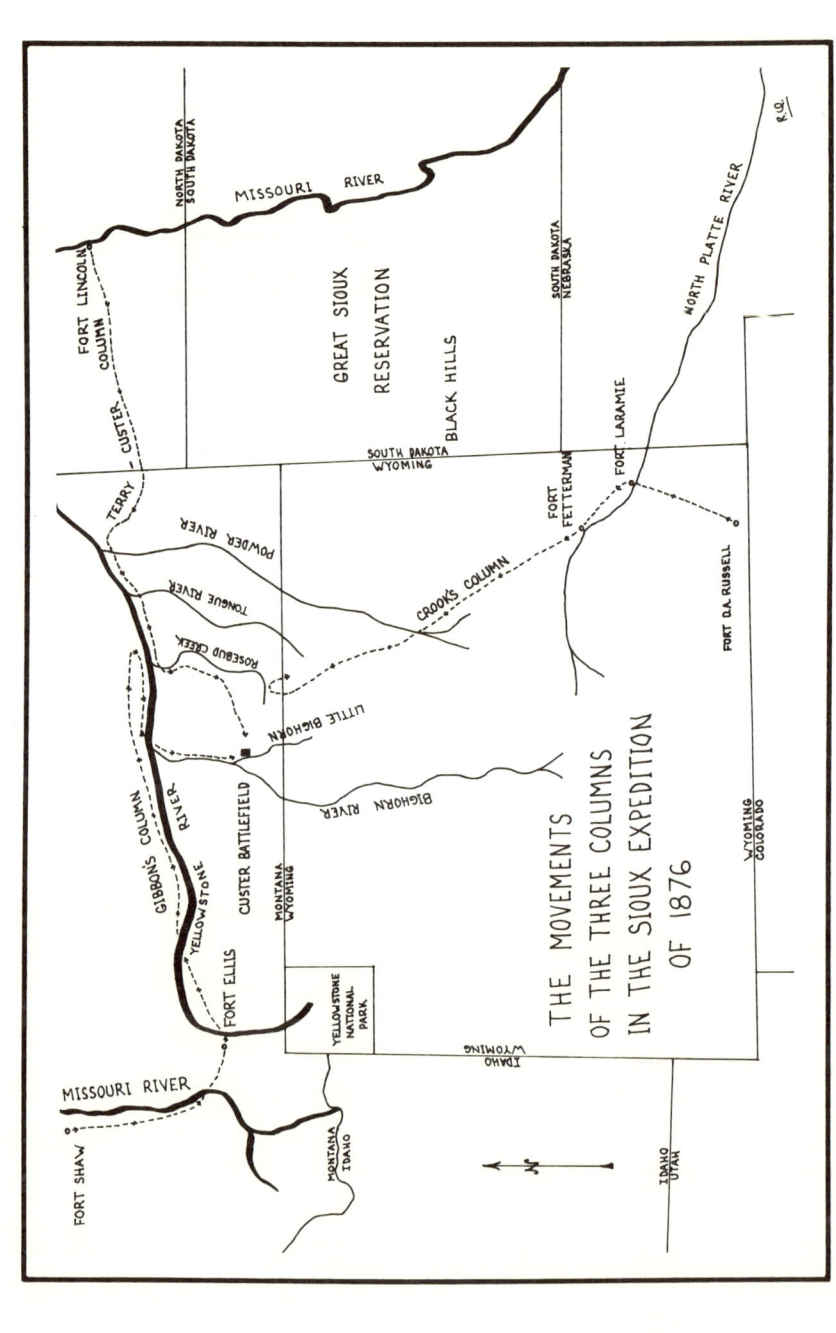

CHAPTER ONE
"Setting the Stage"

It has become popular in our society today to blame the Indian Wars of the last half of the 19th century on the failure of the United States government to honor the provisions of the treaties negotiated with the Indians during that period. The facts, however, do not substantiate this opinion; indeed, the government appears to have fulfulled its obligations under the 1851 and 1868 Fort Laramie treaties in a responsible and fair manner. Unfortunately, the same cannot be said about earlier treaties with other tribes. Treaties are binding upon both parties, and the failure of either party to honor the provisions of a treaty render the agreement null and void.

As a new nation, the United States was destined to move westward in its development. This is a fact which cannot be denied, and those who challenge the morality of this westward expansion fail to consider the parallel fact that the Sioux Nation was migrating west of the Mississippi at the same time — not by treaty arrangement with other tribes, but by relentless and forceful aggression. The lesser tribes living peaceably in the path of this Sioux tidal wave were swept aside and forced to seek out lands in areas far from their homelands.

When the nomadic nature of the Plains Indian is considered, it might appear to many that the use of the term "homelands" is a misnomer. With the possible exception of certain agricultural tribes, such as the Mandans and Hidatsa, the only land ever "owned" by a Plains Indian was the area occupied temporarily by his tepee and his horses. This ownership was always subject to challenge by his enemies, and the retention of his "property" depended entirely upon the "owner's" ability to defend it. Whether he successfully held it or not, the land area was still held temporarily, for the Plains Indian never lived in any one area for any appreciable length of time, particularly in the summer months.

With this in mind it is difficult to understand the claim of the American Indian Movement that the Dacotah or Teton Sioux are the actual owners of that area known as the Black Hills of South Dakota, by right of inheritance and by the terms of a treaty with the United States. They regard the government's seizure of these lands following the Indian Wars as illegal, and demand full restoration of the disputed territory to Sioux ownership.

The facts fail to support this claim. The Dacotah people are not native to the Dakotas, despite the fact that this area now bears their name. The first written mention of the Sioux is to be found in Paul Le Jeune's document entitled *Relation,* published in 1640.[1] At that time, according to Le Jeune, the Sioux were living in Wisconsin and around the headwaters of the Mississippi in northern Minnesota. They were forest people, with a special affinity for the timbered lake region of the upper Midwest, and they had neither horses nor firearms. During the last half of the 18th century, French traders began moving north from their post at St. Louis, Missouri, and they began trading with the Chippewas or Ojibways, bitter enemies of the Sioux. The introduction of firearms tipped the balance of power in favor of the Chippewas and the Sioux were forced to drift westward, up the Minnesota River valley where they remained for over a hundred years.

As late as 1738 the elder La Verendrye, visiting the Mandans

SETTING THE STAGE 21

along the Missouri River in what is now North Dakota, was told by these people that there were no Sioux to the south of them, and that all the Sioux were to the east, from the present Red Lake, Minnesota, to Lake of the Woods where La Verendrye had encountered them in 1732.[2]

When Lewis and Clark passed through the Dakotas in 1804, they reported that only two settlements of Teton Sioux were found along the Missouri River.[3] There was no general migration of Sioux to the western prairies until the middle of the 19th century.[4]

There is evidence that the Sioux knew of the Black Hills long before they migrated to that area. A Sioux Winter Count, dated 1775, mentions that a Dacotah "discovered" the Black Hills at that time and that he found them occupied by the Cheyennes.[5] There is overwhelming evidence that the Cheyennes were there long before the Teton Sioux. The noted historian-geologist, George Bird Grinnell, author of many books on the Cheyennes with whom he lived for many years, said that when the Cheyennes first secured possession of the Black Hills country, an area which included the Little Missouri and the Belle-Fourche-Cheyenne rivers, there were no Sioux there, and that the Sioux came much later.[6]

The Cheyenne warrior, Wooden Leg, told his biographer that he was born in 1858, when his people "were camped by the waters of the Cheyenne River in the Black Hills."[7]

Grinnell, in his books, describes the migration of this tribe from their home on the Missouri River (near the present town of Ft. Pierre, South Dakota) to the Black Hills area and mentions that the Cheyennes found it already occupied by the Kiowas and Comanches.[8] Even the Crow Indians of Montana had ranged as far east as the Black Hills. Plenty Coups, last of the great Crow chiefs said that "the Lacota (Sioux), the Cheyennes and the Arapahoes kept pushing us back, away from the Black Hills."[9]

Apparently the first Sioux to migrate west of the Missouri were the Brule and Ogallala. According to Spotted Tail, chief of the Brules, his branch of the Teton Sioux settled on the White River where it joins the Missouri possibly as early as 1800, and the Ogallalas became their neighbors soon after.[10]

Despite claims of "ownership" there is not one shred of evidence to indicate that *any* Indian tribe actually lived in the Black Hills, although most of them must have hunted there on occasion. To the Indians the Black Hills were the dwelling place of the spirits; individual Indians would spend a few days there as part of religious ceremonies, but no settlements were ever established in the Hills proper.

On September 17, 1851, D.D. Mitchell, Superintendent of Indian Affairs, and Thomas Fitzpatrick, Indian Agent, met as duly appointed agents of the President of the United States, with the Indians "residing south of the Missouri River, east of the Rocky Mountains and north of the lines of Texas and New Mexico"[11] at Fort Laramie, Wyoming. The tribes included the Sioux, Cheyennes, Arapahoes, Crows, Assiniboines, Gros Ventres, Mandans, and Arickaras. Nearly 10,000 Indians attended this meeting, "assembled for the purpose of establishing and confirming peaceful relations" between the various tribes, and between the Indians and whites.[12] Unfortunately, the treaty was never ratified by Congress, and is of interest today only because it established reservations for the various tribes with boundaries mutually acceptable to all parties, and these boundaries, though later modified, formed the basis of the reservation system as it existed during the time of the Indian Wars.

The treaty did provide that the Indians would recognize the right of the government to lay out roads and establish military posts in Indian territory. Both sides promised to maintain peace, and to reimburse the injured party if this peace were violated. The United States agreed to pay an annual indemnity for any damage done to the "flora and fauna" of the area, and as later amended by Congress, to continue this indemnity for a period of fifteen years.

Although the treaty was never ratified it was recognized by the government and every effort was made to uphold it. But the ink was hardly dry on the treaty before the Sioux made it clear that the document was written on the wind and did not apply to them. In the ten years following the signing of the treaty the Sioux appropriated for themselves a portion of the territory which had been granted to the Crows, and at the 1868 treaty parley, they forced the government to deal with *them* in matters pertaining to the part of the Crow reservation which they, the Sioux, had taken by force.

But perhaps the greatest injustice of all was that which was perpetrated against the Cheyenne Indians by the government. Perhaps misled by the obvious strength of the Sioux and ignorant of the true situation, the government granted to the Sioux all of what is now western South Dakota from the Missouri on the east, to the Wyoming border on the west, including the Black Hills, then held by the Cheyennes!

John Stands-In-Timber, late historian of the Cheyennes, wrote: "The Cheyennes understood very little of what was signed at the treaty. Most of the tribes got to keep their usual territory, but the Sioux were given rights to the Black Hills and other country that the Northern Cheyennes claimed. Their home country was the Black Hills."[13]

According to Stands-In-Timber, the famous chief Little Wolf, who later fell into disgrace in his tribe, was blamed for this gross error. Stands-In-Timber wrote: "He signed a treaty without authority that gave most of the old Cheyenne Black Hills country away to the Sioux."[14]

There is little doubt that the Sioux, already pressing westward from the Missouri, would have soon dispossessed the Cheyennes anyway, but this does not alter the fact that the

Black Hills, at the 1851 Treaty, were illegally taken from the Cheyennes and given to the Sioux.

The Fort Laramie Treaty of 1868 is notable chiefly in that it is the only instrument of surrender ever signed by the United States government. It reaffirmed the reservation boundaries of 1851, and then proceeded to submit to all of the demands of the Sioux by agreeing to abandon all the military posts which had been erected along the Bozeman Trail. Without the restraining presence of the military, the Sioux were now free to trespass upon the domain of the Crows and to continue their attacks upon white parties traveling to the Montana gold fields. One indisputable instance of this trespass on the part of the Sioux is that the Battle of the Little Big Horn in southeastern Montana took place well within the boundaries of the *Crow* reservation.

General George Crook, commander of the Department of the Platte, summed up the causes of the Indian Wars in his official report, September 23, 1876, when he said: "It was well known that the Treaty of 1868 has been regarded by the Indians as an instrument binding upon us but not binding on them... it is notorious that, from the date of the treaty to the present, there has been no time that the settlers were free from the very offences laid down" (as provisions of the treaty). "Indians have without interruption, attacked persons at home, murdered and scalped them, stolen their stock, in fact violated every leading feature of the treaty."[15]

It has been claimed that the Black Hills Expedition of 1874, led by General Custer, was a violation of the Fort Laramie Treaty, and the immediate cause of the 1876 Indian Wars. Neither statement is correct. Article 2 of the 1868 Treaty specifically authorizes "such officers, agents, and employees of the government... to enter upon Indian Reservations in discharge of duties enjoined by law."[16] General Sheridan, Commander of the Military District of the Missouri, was well within his rights in ordering the expedition to the Black Hills.

After gold was discovered in the Black Hills, the government attempted to purchase the area from the Sioux, but the negotiations failed simply because the "owners" could not agree among themselves whether to sell or, if they did, what price should be paid.

It was not until after the Sioux Wars of 1876 that negotiations were resumed. This time the government, having broken the back of Indian resistance, held the advantage, and the United States was not in the same conciliatory mood that had marked the 1868 Treaty agreement. The Sioux now stood convicted by their hostile actions of violating that Treaty agreement. Finally, on August 15, 1876, an Agreement was drawn up between the victor and the vanquished re-determining the western boundary of the Great Sioux Reservation to its present limits, some distance *east* of the Black Hills, and "the said Indians do hereby relinquish and cede to the United States all the Territory lying outside the said reservation..."[17] In return, the government agreed to fulfill the other provisions of the 1868 Treaty, such as to provide schools and rations "to assist the said Indians in the work of civilization."

The Treaty of 1868 was dead. It had died at the hands of the Sioux, who had violated every provision relating to the responsibilities which were incumbent upon them as party to it. Their future as a people was now totally in the hands of their conquerors. The Apaches, the Cheyennes, the Nez Perce, and many other tribes which had fought against the government and lost, fared much worse than the Sioux, some of them suffering long term imprisonment. But such are the fortunes of war.

The Agreement of 1876 which revoked the right of the Sioux to any claim upon the Black Hills, might appear to some to be "poetic justice," imperfect, to be sure, for the Hills were never returned to the previous "owners," the Cheyennes. But perhaps Justice prevailed here, too, for the Cheyennes had been willing accomplices of the Sioux in the Wars of 1876 and in the years of depredations that preceded the final outbreak.

Evidence to support the charge that the Sioux — that is, the Lakota or Teton Sioux — had indeed abrogated the terms of the 1851 and 1868 treaties is abundant. Western newspapers pleaded for help, urging the government to take action against the hostiles. Dexter E. Clapp, Agent of the Crow Reservation in Montana, made repeated appeals to Washington for help in repelling the marauding Sioux who apparently considered the Crow reservation as part of their own. In regular letters to the Commissioner of Indian Affairs, Clapp cited attack after attack, to which Crow Indians and civilian employees of the Agency were subjected. Finally, in September 1875, he closed his report with: "I respectfully urge, that such action shall be taken as shall effectively quiet the hostile Indians in the Yellowstone country, and give to the whites peace, and to the Crows opportunity for the progress of civilization."[18]

Nor was this an isolated complaint; similar reports of Sioux aggression poured into Washington from the Platte to the Missouri, and from the prairies of the Dakotas to the mountains of Montana. Finally, in desperation, the Bureau of Indian Affairs turned the matter over to the War Department for military action, and the stage was set for the Sioux Expedition of 1876.

The task of organizing the Expedition was given to Lieutenant General Phil Sheridan, Commander of the military district of Missouri. He decided to move his forces into action before the Spring of 1876, hoping to catch the hostiles snowbound and lethargic from the cold, late winter. To accomplish this, he planned a three-pronged pincer movement involving troops of the Department of Dakota (which included the territory of Montana) under Brigadier General Alfred H. Terry, and the Department of the Platte, commanded by Brigadier General George Crook. The Dakota forces were two prongs of Sheridan's "fork:" the Montana contingent, headed by Colonel (Brevet Major General) John Gibbon from Fort Shaw on the Sun River and Fort Ellis, near Bozeman, and the Dakota contingent, commanded by Lieutenant Colonel (Brevet Major General) George Armstrong Custer from Fort Abraham Lincoln, near Bismarck.

An exasperating combination of politics and bad weather made it impossible for the Dakota contingent to take to the field, and on March 1, 1876, General Crook marched out from Fort Fetterman, Wyoming, with ten companies of cavalry, two companies of infantry, and a host of attached guides and packers, numbering about one thousand men.

Crook's command marched in a northerly direction, cutting over from Powder River to Goose Creek, a tributary of the Tongue, then over the Montana border along the Tongue River. Just below the mouth of Hanging Woman Creek, Crook crossed over to the east towards the valley of another Tongue tributary, Otter Creek. Here the scouts reported Indian pony tracks, and Crook ordered Colonel John J. Reynolds to follow the trail with six companies of the cavalry, to strike the Indians where he found them, and then to report back to the main column which he would find encamped on Lodge Pole Creek the following night. Reynolds was told to destroy everything he found — Indians, ponies, tepees, and everything else capable of providing sustenance to the hostiles.

At daybreak the next morning, March 17, Reynolds found a village of about one hundred lodges (approximately six hundred Indians) just above the mouth of the Little Powder, on the west bank of the Powder River. He ordered one battalion to charge into the village while the second battalion dismounted to cover the attack from a line of bluffs bordering the north end of the village. The third battalion was then to follow the first, concentrating on capturing the pony herd and destroying the camp. As the leading companies moved in on their charge, the

Indians were alerted and came out to meet them, forcing the troops to dismount and hold their position in a skirmish line. However, the battalion detailed to cover the attack from the bluffs was delayed in reaching its objective — perhaps failed to reach their objective would be more accurate, for the position they took was too far back of the attacking force to lend any effective support. Major Anson Mills then moved his troops forward dismounted, and forced the hostiles to abandon their camp. The scouts then moved in under Mills' protective cover and rounded up a great number of the Indian ponies while the troops set fire to the village. Unfortunately, the destruction of the village failed to take into consideration the needs of the attacking forces. Meat, buffalo robes, and other paraphernalia that could have been placed to good use by the troops was destroyed. Three or four soldiers were killed, and at least one was seriously wounded while holding the hostiles at bay. Suddenly Reynolds broke off the engagement and ordered his troops to retire, leaving the wounded and the bodies of the slain to the tender mercies of the hostiles. Lieutenant Bourke of the 3rd Cavalry Regiment later wrote that "the movement was carried out so precipitately that we practically abandoned the victory to the savages."[19]

Colonel Reynolds and his men then marched southward up the valley of the Powder and encamped just south of the Montana border. The next morning a number of the Indians who had followed the troops raided the stolen pony herd and succeeded in recapturing a large number of their mounts. Reynolds refused to allow his men to pursue them, intent only on rejoining General Crook, which was accomplished about noon that day.

The troops at the time believed they were fighting the Sioux under Crazy Horse, and many later writers have perpetuated this error. Although three or four Ogallala lodges were present in the village, it was principally a Cheyenne camp. Wooden

Leg, the young Cheyenne warrior who was present that day said that the Cheyennes moved northeastward after Reynolds' attack and joined Crazy Horse and his Ogallalas on a creek east of the Powder River.

General Crook was highly displeased over the conduct of his regimental commander and later preferred charges against him and two of Reynolds' battalion commanders. For the present there was nothing left for Crook to do but to return to Fort Fetterman, make his report to Sheridan, and await further orders. The planned winter campaign was aborted, and though Reynolds' battle with the Cheyennes was not really a defeat, it was, as Bourke implied, no victory.

On the same day that Reynolds attacked the Cheyennes on Powder River, March 17, General Gibbon's Montana column set out from Fort Shaw on the Sun River, marching south to Fort Ellis where he picked up additional troops and, from Crow Agency, a number of Crow Indian scouts. His column now included four companies of the 2nd Cavalry Regiment, six companies of the 7th Infantry Regiment, and one company of the 18th Infantry, a total of 27 officers, 426 enlisted men, and 23 Crow scouts. Gibbon set out early in April proceeding eastward along the Yellowstone River, and was in place opposite the mouth of the Rosebud River (a few miles east of the present town of Forsyth, Montana) late in May. The march had been fairly uneventful, marked only by a few encounters with roving bands of hostiles. While encamped there, Gibbon received a dispatch informing him that the Dakota column from Fort A. Lincoln was now on the way.

The Dakota column got underway on May 17 with the expedition commander, General Terry, accompanying the troops under the command of General Custer. The column was led by twelve companies of the 7th Cavalry Regiment, three companies of the 20th Infantry, a platoon of Gatling guns, a crew of packers, and nearly forty Indian scouts, mostly

Arickara. Chief of the civilian scouts was "Lonesome Charley" Reynolds, and the contingent included the Jackson brothers (half Sioux) and a black man, Isaiah Dorman.

On June 9 the column reached the Powder River where a supply depot was established and much of the excess equipment, including the cavalry sabers, was left here along with the 7th's Regimental Band.

A reconnaissance of the area to the south was ordered by General Terry and the task was assigned to the right wing of the regiment, companies C, E, F, G, I and L, commanded by Custer's second-in-command, Brevet Colonel Marcus A. Reno, the only major present. Reno was ordered to scout to the south and west, ending up at the mouth of the Tongue River. Terry then boarded the supply steamer, *Far West*, and proceeded to the Tongue to await Reno's report. Custer, leading the remainder of the troops, proceeded along the Yellowstone to join Terry at the mouth of Tongue River.

Reno's reconnaissance led him south to the mouth of the Little Powder, then westward across the headwaters of Mizpah and Pumpkin creeks, to the Tongue. From there Reno continued westward to the Rosebud River, moving upstream a few miles before turning back and heading for the river's mouth. On reaching the Yellowstone Reno halted the command and sent word to General Terry that he had discovered a large Indian trail on the Rosebud. He was ordered to remain there until the rest of the regiment and the supply steamer could join him.

While the troops under Crook, Gibbon and Custer were in motion, so were the Indians. The clearest account of their movements is given by the Cheyenne, Wooden Leg, and his description of their wanderings enables us to follow them from the Powder River to the final battle on the Little Big Horn.[20]

After the fight on the Powder the Cheyennes moved northeasterly and joined Crazy Horse and his Ogallalas far up a creek east of the Powder, arriving there four days later, about March 21. From there the hostiles moved together, traveling about fifty miles east in a northeasterly direction to a stream that flows westward into the Powder, just east of Chalk Butte. Here they joined the Uncpapas and Minneconjous. It was now about March 24, and they remained there about five or six days. Wooden Leg tells us that the increased number of people and horses could not stay in one place long because of the quick depletion of grazing, so they decided to move northward to the head of the next stream flowing into the east side of the Powder, the Cheyennes in the lead, the Ogallalas, Minneconjous and Uncpapas following in that order. They remained in their new location for three days before moving to the north, traveling all night. Again they encamped, this time at the upper region of the next tributary of the Powder where they were joined by the Sans Arcs. By this time the Cheyenne lodges had increased to a total of fifty. Three or four days later the hostiles moved northwestward to another tributary on the east side of the Powder. Wooden Leg believed that the Blackfeet Sioux, some Assiniboines, Santees and Brules all joined here, coming from the north side of the Yellowstone. It was here that the Cheyenne chief, Lame White Man, and a large number of other Cheyennes joined the growing hostile force.

From their camp on the Powder River, the Indians moved directly westward over the hill country. Wooden Leg believed they camped in two or three places between the Powder and the Tongue, one day spent in each camp. When they reached the Tongue they were joined by Dirty Moccasin and a large band of Cheyennes which doubled their number. From the Tongue River they continued moving west, stopping for four or five days at what Wooden leg called "the first creek of importance west of Tongue River," known to the Indians as Wood Creek. Their time here was spent in hunting buffalo and other game which was plentiful, while the herds of horses found adequate grazing. From Wood Creek the Indians moved westward again to the upper part of Sioux Creek, spending a day there, then they proceeded westward to the Rosebud. Wooden Leg's estimate of the date they arrived was about the middle of May. Dr. Marquis appended a note here, stating that "Thomas H. Leforge and his Crow scouts (with Gibbon) learned that the hostile Indians arrived on the Rosebud about May 19, 1876. They observed a great camp there on May 25th."[21]

This first Rosebud camp was about 7 or 8 miles south of the Yellowstone River. Wooden Leg said that more Cheyennes joined them at this camp on the east side of the Rosebud and that they all remained there about seven days before moving to a new site about twelve miles upstream (south).

We get some idea of the size of the camp in this new location. The Cheyenne circle was a mile and a half or more south of the rear-guard Uncpapas, and the other tribes were between them. After only one night at this campsite the Indians moved on to the south along the Rosebud valley for another twelve or fifteen miles, and the next morning they were on the move again.

Their fourth camp on the Rosebud can be more easily identified. It was "at or above" the junction of the old road from Colstrip with the present-day road that follows the Rosebud River. Wooden Leg further identifies it by stating that the Cheyenne camp circle, furthest south, was at the mouth of Greenleaf Creek. Food was growing scarce and Sioux hunting parties were busy roaming the hills west of the Rosebud for buffalo. Three days after arriving at this camp, Wooden Leg was one of eleven Cheyennes who set out toward the Tongue River to the south east as a hunting and scouting party.

The results of this Cheyenne reconnaissance were to have a decisive effect on the plans of the military forces and would be the first link in the chain of events that would culminate in the Battle of the Little Big Horn.

CHAPTER TWO
"Where the Sister Saved Her Brother"

On May 29, General Crook, fully recuperated from the Powder River fight, set out once again on the trail of the hostiles. Scouts had reported that the Indians were encamped on the Rosebud River moving south, so Crook marched from his headquarters at Fort Fetterman with a large force of cavalry, infantry, and a number of civilian packers and teamsters. At Clear Creek he was joined by a group of miners who were on their way to the Montana gold fields. The column then continued north toward Goose Creek where Crook hoped to meet with his Indian scouts, but the column apparently lost its way, and on June 6 Crook found himself at the mouth of Prairie Dog Creek. Three days later the column was attacked by a small band of Cheyennes, but the cavalry had no difficulty driving them off. Crook then moved his command back to Goose Creek and encamped on the site of present-day Sheridan, Wyoming. Here, on June 14, he was joined by a large contingent of Crow and Shoshone Indian scouts, and Crook was now ready to move against the hostiles in force, with over thirteen hundred men under his command.[1]

That force consisted of five companies of the Second Cavalry Regiment and ten companies of the Third Cavalry commanded by Lt. Col. William B. Royall, two companies of the Fourth Infantry and three companies of the Ninth Infantry, commanded by Major Alex Chambers. In addition to the military units, there were eighty-six Shoshone and one-hundred seventy-six Crow Indian scouts, three guides and interpreters, sixty-five miners, five newspaper correspondents, and as noted above, a number of civilian packers and teamsters to handle the supply wagons and pack train.[2]

It was a formidable force, apparently capable of meeting a like number of Indians and dispatching them with ease, and by the evening of June 16, the command reached the south tributaries of the south fork of the Rosebud, covering a distance of nearly forty miles. Here they made camp, resting up for the next day's march.[3]

On June 8, while the troops were resting at the mouth of Prairie Dog Creek, Wooden Leg and his ten companions discovered them. After observing the soldiers for some time, the Cheyenne hunting party rode back toward the Rosebud to warn the others that soldiers were headed in their direction. They arrived at the main camp the next day and reported. The chiefs of the various tribes met in council to discuss the disturbing news. Wooden Leg tells us that the Cheyenne chiefs selected Little Hawk and two or three others to find the soldier camp and observe its movements. Apparently there were scouts from one or more of the Sioux tribes in the party and they all left immediately. The camp then moved up the Rosebud valley about ten miles to the mouth of Davis Creek, a small tributary of the Rosebud rising in the Wolf Mountains, a chain of hills which form the divide between the Rosebud and Little Big Horn valley. Wooden Leg believes they stayed in this camp more than one day, then moved west along Davis Creek.[4]

Indian testimony confirms that the destination of the Indians was near the headwaters of the Little Big Horn River.[5] The simplest way to reach that destination was to follow the Rosebud to its source, then to cross the divide to the Little Big Horn. It is necessary to study the map of this area to note that

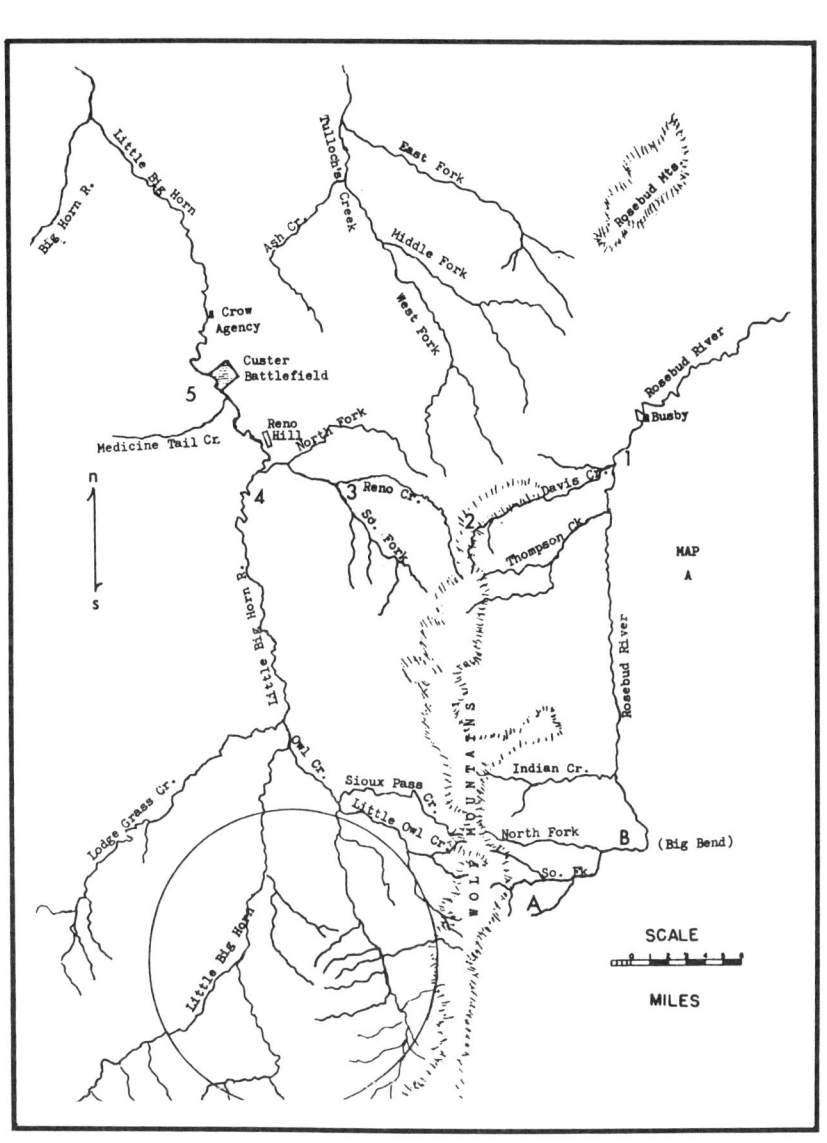

the Rosebud, looking at it from its mouth on the Yellowstone River, extends south by southwest to a point about fifteen miles from the Wyoming border, then turns sharply to the west at what is known as the "Big Bend." About three miles west of this sharp bend in the stream, the Rosebud divides into the south and north forks which form its headwaters. From this point it is only three miles further west to Little Owl Creek, a tributary of the Little Big Horn. A little south of this juncture is the area which has been described as "Indian Paradise," for it is fed by numerous springs and streams, and at that time abounded in wild game and lush grasslands.

The report of the scouts that soldiers were moving north toward the Rosebud meant that the intended route of the Indians had been blocked to them, and it was this fact that led to the decision of the chiefs to leave the Rosebud and move immediately to the west following Davis Creek. This route would take them to the divide of the Wolf Mountains, and from there they could move safely down to the Little Big Horn valley, twelve miles to the west.

It might be useful here to refer to the map shown on page 35. The number "1" indicates the last camp of the hostiles on the Rosebud before turning west. The large circle at the bottom left of the map shows the general area of the Indians' intended destination.

On June 15 the hostiles camped near the divide (No. "2" on the map), spent the night there, then moved down the west slope of the mountains following what is now known as Reno Creek, a tributary of the Little Big Horn. At the junction of the two forks of this stream they made their camp. (No. "3" on the map). It was here that Little Hawk and his scouts found them and reported that the soldiers were now on the upper forks of the Rosebud ("A" on the map), about twenty-five miles, as the "crow flies," from the camp on Reno Creek. Again the chiefs met in council to discuss Little Hawk's information, and

Wooden Leg tells us that they advised the young men to "leave the soldiers alone unless they attack us." The advice went unheeded, and under cover of darkness about 200 Cheyennes and 800 Sioux slipped out of the camp, some riding along the south fork of Reno Creek, and others crossing over the divide to the Rosebud.[6] Early on the morning of June 17, they found the troops just west of the Big Bend of the Rosebud ("B" on the map).

General Crook and his command had reached the Rosebud on June 16, encamping at the headwaters of the south fork of that stream. The following morning the column began the march down the Rosebud, presumably to strike the Indian village which was thought to be near the mouth of Indian Creek, about five miles north of the Big Bend.

At about 8:00 or 8:30 a.m., the troops halted to rest on both sides of the creek, the cavalry in the vanguard, followed by the infantry, the pack train and the scouts.[7]

The terrain in this part of the upper Rosebud valley has been described as similar to an amphitheatre, with high bluffs on the south sloping down toward the river, then a wide valley, and on the north side of the valley, a series of ridges.

Here the troops relaxed, some making campfires to boil coffee, the horses were unbridled, unsaddled and set out to graze. General Crook and his adjutant spent the time playing cards.

Fortunately some of the Crow scouts were occupying their time more constructively by doing their job. Some distance north of Crook's bivouac the scouts met up with the advance forces of the hostiles moving toward Crook's position. A few shots were fired, then the Crows raced back to the Rosebud to alert the command. Only the infantry was prepared for immediate action and they were rushed forward in a line facing the ridges on the north side of the stream while the cavalry began securing their horses. But it was the Crow and Shoshone scouts that saved the day, holding off the hostiles until the troops were ready.

The early fighting was "hit and run," charges and counter-charges. Finally Crook was able to get his forces in action, but the hostiles provided no stationary targets. Soon the fighting began to spread out to the east and to the west and the soldiers were spread out on a three mile front with a battalion of cavalry on the right led by Major Anson Mills, captain of "M" Company, Third Cavalry, and the others, under Col. Royall, on the left. The miners, whose marksmanship proved invaluable, were generally located in the middle with the packers. There are some reports of hand to hand combat, but this was rare. The superb horsemanship of the hostiles enabled them to charge and withdraw before the troops could respond, disappearing among the many ridges and small ravines.

Crook was determined to seize the initiative which up to this point had been held by the hostiles. Believing that their village was only a few miles downstream from the Big Bend, he ordered Mills to seek out and attack that village, forcing the warriors to retreat in order to protect their families. A battalion of four companies of the cavalry led by Mills then set off down the Rosebud valley toward Indian Creek.

Mills and his men rode southeast into the valley, then north toward the mouth of Indian Creek where the valley narrows into what some have called Rosebud Canyon or "the Gorge," an extreme exaggeration. Actually, the broad valley narrows to about 150 yards, and the cavalry seems to have had no difficulty reaching Indian Creek. Shortly after arriving there, Mills received orders from General Crook to return to the battlefield immediately to support Col. Royall, whose position had become precarious. Mills decided to take a short-cut to the southwest which brought him back to the field behind the Indian lines. The appearance of troops at their rear disconcerted the hostiles and they broke off the engagement, heading back to Reno Creek.[8]

It is estimated that a thousand Sioux and Cheyenne warriors participated in the Battle of the Rosebud. Casualties were remarkably light, considering the total number of combatants. Crook reported that nine soldiers were killed, but other estimates run as high as fifty-seven. Indian losses were probably about thirty.

There were acts of heroism on both sides, but one incident described by the Cheyennes is especially noteworthy. Chief Comes In Sight, fighting on the eastern end of the battlefield, had his horse shot out from under him. His sister, Buffalo Calf Road Woman who had accompanied the warriors and participated in some of the fighting, saw her brother's predicament and daringly rode to his rescue. Comes In Sight was able to jump on her horse behind her and the two escaped. It was this incident that inspired the Cheyennes to call this battle, "the place where the sister saved her brother."[9]

General Crook, with most of his ammunition gone and a number of wounded men, decided to return to his base on Goose Creek. He had found the Indians much stronger and more aggressive than he had believed possible, a fact that others would also learn only a week later. Crook's decision to return to base rather than pursue the hostiles has been the subject of some criticism, but considering his own position only, apart from the role he was intended to play in the overall plans of General Sheridan, his decision was justified.

It is unfortunate, however, that after returning to his base and replenishing his supplies and ammunition, he did not set out again. If he had, he would have found that the Indian trail was farther north than he had believed, and that it turned away from the Rosebud toward the Little Big Horn. Even allowing a day of rest for his troops at the Goose Creek camp, Crook could easily have reached Davis Creek (where the Indians turned west) by June 24. Had he done so, he would have met Custer's regiment at that point and together they could have continued their pursuit of the hostiles with a force of nearly two thousand soldiers, scouts and other personnel. Although Crook's exact position could not have been pinpointed by General Terry, it *was* known that he was south of the Dakota column, and Terry must have presumed that a junction of the two forces would take place somewhere in that vicinity. Failing that, Crook could at least have sent a courier to Terry informing him of what had happened. Such information would have altered Terry's own plans considerably. As it turned out, Crook was now out of the fight and would not figure into General Sheridan's plans again until the mopping-up campaign that would begin in July.

CHAPTER THREE
"The March up the Rosebud"

It was June 19 when Terry and Custer, encamped on Tongue River, received Reno's report of his reconnaissance. After sending Reno orders to wait at the mouth of the Rosebud, Terry again boarded the steamer, proceeding west, while Custer and the rest of the regiment marched along the south bank of the Yellowstone, reaching the Rosebud at noon on June 21.

At a conference aboard the supply steamer, Terry, Gibbon and Custer discussed Reno's discovery of the large Indian trail leading south. We have a correspondent's account of this meeting which appeared in the July 8, 1876, edition of the *New York Herald:*

"A consultation was held with Generals Gibbon and Custer and then General Terry definitely fixed upon the plan of action. It was believed the Indians were on the head of the Rosebud, or over on the Little Horn, a divide of about fifteen miles separating the two streams. It was announced by General Terry that General Custer's column would strike the blow and General Gibbon and his men received the decision without a murmur.

"There was great rivalry between the two columns and each wanted to be in at the death. General Gibbon's cavalry had been in the field since the 22nd of last February, herding and watching these Indians and the infantry had been in the field and on the march since early last March. They had come to regard the Yellowstone Indians as their peculiar property and have worked and waited five months until the Indians could be concentrated and General Crook and Terry get into position to prevent their escape. The Montana column felt disappointed when they learned that they were not to be present at the final capture of the great village but General Terry's reasons for affording the honor of the attack to General Custer were good ones. First Custer had all cavalry and could pursue if they attempted to escape, while Gibbon's column was half infantry, and in rapid marching in approaching the village, as well as pursuing the Indians after the fight, General Gibbon's cavalry and infantry must become separated and the strength of the column be weakened. Second, General Custer's column was numerically stronger than Gibbon's and General Terry desired the strongest column to strike the Indians; so it was decided that Custer's men were, as usual, to have the post of honor and the officers and men of the Montana column cheered them and bade them God-speed."

Lt. James Bradley, 7th Infantry, and Gibbon's chief of scouts, noted in his journal the evening of June 21: "It is understood that if Custer arrives first he is at liberty to attack at once if he deems prudent."[1]

The result of the conference aboard the "Far West" was the now famous "orders" which Terry issued to Custer through his adjutant.

There has been so much controversy over these orders that a review of them is necessary. The letter reads as follows:

Camp at mouth of Rosebud
River, Montana Territory
June 22, 1876

Lieutenant Colonel Custer,
7th Cavalry
Colonel:
    The Brigadier General Commanding directs that, as soon as your regiment can be made ready for the march, you will proceed up the

THE MARCH UP THE ROSEBUD

Rosebud in pursuit of the Indians whose trail was discovered by Major Reno a few days since. It is, of course, impossible to give you any definite instructions in regard to this movement, and were it not impossible to do so the Dept. Commander places too much confidence in your zeal, energy and ability to wish to impose upon you precise orders which might hamper your action when nearly in contact with the enemy.

He will, however, indicate to you his own views of what your action should be, and he desires that you should conform to them unless you shall see sufficient reason for departing from them. He thinks that you should proceed up the Rosebud until you ascertain definitely the direction in which the trail above spoken of leads. Should it be found (as it appears almost certain that it will be found) to turn towards the Little Horn, he thinks that you should still proceed southward, perhaps as far as the headwaters of the Tongue, and then turn towards the Little Horn, feeling constantly, however, to your left, so as to preclude the possibility of the escape of the Indians to the South or Southeast by passing around your left flank.

The column of Colonel Gibbon is now in motion for the mouth of the Big Horn. As soon as it reaches that point it will cross the Yellowstone and move up at least as far as the forks of the Big and Little Horns. Of course its future movements must be controlled by circumstances as they arise, but it is hoped that the Indians, if upon the Little Horn, may be so nearly enclosed by the two columns that their escape will be impossible.

The Department Commander desires that upon your way up the Rosebud you should thoroughly examine the upper part of Tulloch's Creek, and that you should endeavor to send a scout to Colonel Gibbon's column with information of the result of your examination. The lower part of this Creek will be examined by a detachment from Col. Gibbon's command.

The supply steamer will be pushed up the Big Horn as far as the forks if the river is found to be navigable for that distance, and the Dept. Commander, who will accompany the column of Col. Gibbon, desires you to report to him there not later than the time for which your troops are rationed, unless in the meantime you receive further orders.

Very respectfully,
Your obedient servant,
(Signed) E.W. Smith,
Captain 18th Infantry

Were these "orders" or "suggestions?" The obvious answer is that they were both. The verbs "directs" and "desires" definitely indicate orders; the words "he thinks" are suggestions.

The letter begins with an order: "The Brigadier General Commanding directs that, as soon as your regiment can be made ready for the march, you will proceed up the Rosebud in pursuit of the Indians whose trail was discovered by Major Reno a few days since."

In obedience to that order, the 7th Cavalry passed in review before Generals Terry, Gibbon and Custer at noon, June 22, and began their march up the Rosebud, their commanding officer joining them after a few words of farewell to Terry and Gibbon. The column found the Indian trail entering the Rosebud valley from the east about eight miles from the Rosebud's mouth, and followed it until about 4:00 p.m. It must be remembered that all the clock times refer to what was called "Chicago time" or, as it is better known today, Central Standard time. They had traveled a total of twelve miles on that first day's march, and the command went into bivouac for the night.

Later that night Custer met with his officers, and after a few housekeeping rules about the order of the march, he shared with them his views of what lay ahead. Lt. Edward Godfrey of "K" Company said that Custer "took particular pains to impress upon the officers his reliance upon their judgment, discretion, and loyalty."[2] Brevet Col. Frederick Benteen, senior captain of the regiment, said that Custer gave "a few excellent general orders as to what should be done by each troop of the regiment in case of an attack on our bivouac at any time."[3] Lt. Winfield S. Edgerly, an officer of Captain Weir's "D" Company, said later that the substance of Custer's talk was "that there was no doubt of the presence of a considerable number of hostile Indians within striking distance, that in all probability it would take hard riding to catch them, that he believed they could be overtaken and whipped, that if any troops could accomplish these objects the 7th Cavalry could, and that he hoped we would be successful, and soon be marching back to Fort A. Lincoln."[4]

Edgerly went on the say: "It is important to state here that the general belief shared by Generals Terry, Gibbon and Custer, was that the hostile Indians could not assemble more than 800 warriors, with the possibilities in favor of a lesser number."[5]

This figure had come to the field commanders from the War Department, based on the number of Indians reported absent from their reservations by agents of the Bureau of Indian affairs. As General Sherman admitted in his Official Report of 1876, "Up to the moment of Custer's defeat there was nothing, official or private, to justify an officer to expect that any detachment would encounter more than five hundred or eight hundred warriors."

Unfortunately, General Crook's report of the number of hostiles that faced him on the Rosebud the week before, had not been communicated to the field commanders of the Dakota and Montana columns. These modest estimates of the enemy strength would rise slightly as the column progressed along the march and the scouts found new trails entering the main Indian trail from the east, but at no time before the troops were committed to action on June 25 would these estimates reach even half of the actual number of the hostiles' fighting strength, although at the "Officers' Call" on the night of the first day's march, Lt. Godfrey reported later that Custer "thought, judging from the number of lodge-fires reported by Reno, that we might meet at least a thousand warriors."[6]

The march was resumed at 5:00 o'clock the next morning and about two hours later the command reached the first campsite of the Indians. They continued their trek up the

Rosebud until 5:00 p.m., having covered about thirty-three miles. Col. Benteen, in his story of the battle, said he decided that night to add to the regular "bill of fare" by catching fish with a seine in the tiny stream. Apparently this was a bad night for the troops as Benteen reported that there "were myriads of mosquitoes" under the mulberry bush he had chosen for his rest.[7]

Custer had told Terry that he would try to average thirty miles a day, but in the day and a half that had ended, the column had marched only a total of forty-five miles.

The next morning, June 24, the regiment was on the move again, setting out at 5:00 o'clock. As the meandering Rosebud turned to the west-southwest, it drew closer to the easternmost forks of Tullock's Creek. Terry's instructions to Custer included this directive: "The Department Commander desires that on your way up the Rosebud you should thoroughly examine the upper part of Tulloch's Creek, and that you should endeavor to send a scout through to Colonel Gibbon's column with information of the result of your examination. The lower part of this creek will be examined by a detachment from Colonel Gibbon's command."

It was precisely for this purpose that George Herendeen, a civilian scout attached to Gibbon's command, had been assigned to the 7th Cavalry. There has been considerable criticism of Custer for not complying with this order. Major Brisbin, commanding the cavalry with Gibbon's column and one of Custer's most severe critics, claimed that Herendeen came to Custer and said it was time for him to scout Tullock's, but that Custer ignored him.[8] That story does not agree with Herendeen's own account, published in the New York Herald in January 1878: "On the morning of the 24th we broke camp at 5 o'clock and continued following the trail up the stream. Soon after starting Custer, who was in advance with Bouyer, called me to him and told me to get ready, he thought he would send me and Charley Reynolds to the head of Tullock's Fork to take a look. I told the General it was not time yet, as we were travelling in the direction of the head of Tullock, and I could only follow his trail. I called Bouyer, who was a little ahead back and asked him if I was not correct in my statement to the General, and he said 'Yes; further up on Rosebud we would come opposite a gap, and then we could cut across and strike the Tullock in about fifteen miles' ride.' Custer said, 'All right; I could wait.'"[9]

There is no indication that Herendeen ever returned to tell Custer that the "gap" had been reached, and apparently the subject never came up again. It seems most likely that Custer had indeed ordered Herendeen to scout the Tullock, but in deference to the scout's more precise knowledge of the terrain, had left the time of compliance up to him.

Lt. Edgerly, not aware of Herendeen's account of this incident, said: "Great stress was laid by some upon the fact that Tulloch's Creek was not thoroughly examined, but I believe that with the same orders and conditions, General Terry or any other good soldier would have done just what General Custer did. I consider the situation similar to this hypothetical case: The Post Commander orders me to arrest a murderer who is at large in the garrison. He directs me to the Q.M. shops, then to the Post Exchange, and says he thinks I will find him at one of these places. On my way to the shops I see the criminal in G company quarters. Is there any question as to my duty? Certainly not. I should disregard the portion of the order that I knew to be useless and arrest the man. So in this case."[10]

Edgerly's comments suggest that the troops knew very well they were following the main trail of the Indians, and Lt. Godfrey, commanding "K" Company, substantiates that opinion: "We made many long halts, so as not to get ahead of the scouts, who seemed to be doing their work thoroughly, giving special attention to the right, toward Tulloch's Creek, the valley of which was in general view from the divide. Once or twice signal smokes were reported in that direction, but investigation did not confirm the reports."[11]

In his letter of instructions, Terry informed Custer that "The supply steamer will be pushed up the Big Horn as far as the forks of the river if found to be navigable for that distance, and the Department Commander, who will accompany the column of Colonel Gibbon, desires you to report to him there not later than the time for which your troops are rationed, unless in the meantime you receive further orders."

Subsequent to the battle, Terry's report to General Sheridan concluded with this phrase: "I send in another dispatch a copy of my written orders to Custer, but these were supplemented by the distinct understanding that Gibbon could not get to the Little Big Horn before the evening of the 26th."[12] On the face of it, this appears to be nothing more than informing Custer of Gibbon's approximate position on that date. This seemingly innocuous phrase was soon seized upon by some of Custer's critics as meaning that Custer was not supposed to engage the hostiles until that date, but that in his haste to garner all the "glory" for himself, he deliberately attacked a day early without waiting for Gibbon's support.

Godfrey tells us, "There could not have been any understanding, as contended by some, that the two commands of Custer and Gibbon were to meet at or near the mouth of the Little Big Horn on June 26th."[13]

The reason is obvious; at the time Terry issued his orders to Custer no one knew where the Indians would be found, or even if they would be found at all. Terry's only reference to a future date is in this phrase: (The Department Commander) "desires you to report to him there (at the mouth of the Little Big Horn) not later than the time for which your troops are rationed, unless in the meantime you receive further orders."

And when was that? Again, Godfrey supplies the answer; as a troop commander, he was present at the time Custer shared his instructions with his officers. Godfrey tells us, "We were to transport, on our pack-mules, fifteen days rations." When some of the officers complained about this, Custer left it to their discretion, but told them to bear in mind "we will follow the trail for fifteen days unless we catch them before that time expires, no matter how far it may take us from our base of supplies."[14]

Fifteen days from June 21 or 22 would be either July 5 or 6, and by that time the troops could have been widely separated. As Godfrey remarked, "It is an absurdity to think that the two commands, of 700 and 400, separated by from fifty to one-hundred miles, could coordinate their movements in that open country and hold the hostiles for a co-operative attack."[15]

Early the next morning, June 24, the troops were on the move again, marching 28 miles and making bivouac near the present town of Busby, Montana, on the Cheyenne Reservation. Many of the hostiles' campsites were passed along the way and the trail, in Lt. Edgerly's words, became "fresher and fresher." That night, about 9:30, the officers were called to Custer's tent and were told that the column would resume the march at 11:00 o'clock.

The Crow scouts, who had been working ahead of the column, returned to Custer with the startling news that the hostiles had left the Rosebud valley and had turned sharply to the right up Davis Creek, heading west toward the Little Big Horn! This had to be a totally unexpected development. Custer's orders from Terry had said: "Should it [the trail] be found (as it appears almost certain that it will be found) to turn towards the Little Horn, he [Terry] thinks that you should still proceed southward, perhaps as far as the headwaters of the Tongue, and then turn towards the Little Horn, feeling constantly, however, to your left, so as to preclude the possibility of the escape of the Indians to the South or Southeast by passing around your left flank."

In discussing the probable destination of the Indians, General Terry — undoubtedly aided by the Crow scouts who were now on their home ground — had pinpointed the intended route of the Indians with incredible accuracy.[16] If they had followed the Rosebud to its source, as Terry believed they would do, they would *have* to "turn towards the Little Horn," because that is what the river does! Only a clear understanding of the topography of this area makes the latter part of Terry's directive logical, that if the trail turned to the Little Big Horn, Custer should continue moving south, "perhaps as far as the headwaters of the Tongue," for both the Tongue and the Little Big Horn rise in the Big Horn Mountains of Wyoming. But neither Terry nor Custer knew that General Crook had effectively blocked the Rosebud the week before, forcing the Indians to find another route to their destination. That route was at least twenty miles north of the point where the Indians, following the Rosebud, would turn to the right towards the Little Big Horn.

Much has been said of Custer's supposed "disobedience of orders" in following the Indian trail up Davis Creek. What has not been said is that Terry's order was predicated upon the belief that the Indians would stay on the Rosebud, and certainly they would have done so had it not been for Crook's presence at the Big Bend. Once the Indians left the Rosebud where they did, this portion of Terry's orders was no longer relevant. General Terry, speaking of Gibbon's march to the forks of the Big and Little Horns, had said, "Of course its future movements must be controlled by circumstances as they arise." That was exactly the situation now faced by Custer. He had no choice but to follow the trail, for his orders clearly directed him to "proceed up the Rosebud in pursuit of the

Indians." The reference to the Rosebud was merely informational, for that was where the trail had been discovered. The imperative phrase of this directive was that Custer was to *pursue the Indians,* and to proceed up the Rosebud from this point would be to march *away* from the Indians, an unthinkable maneuver never intended by Terry. It was essential now to determine the direction in which the Indians were heading. When they reached the Little Big Horn, would they turn south to the headwaters? Or would they turn north? The latter possibility would put the Indians and the Montana column on a collision course, for Gibbon was expected to reach the mouth of the Little Big Horn on June 26, and it requires little imagination what would have happened to Gibbon's forces, numbering far less than Custer's, if the Indians struck the Montana column alone.

This unexpected development was something that Terry and Gibbon needed to know. Had it been possible, Custer surely would have dispatched a messenger to Terry, but no purpose could be served by that until Custer knew the location of the Indians — the direction they were going — and the only way to learn that was to follow them.

The column resumed the march at 11:30 that night, moving up Davis Creek, for Custer felt it necessary to reach the divide of the Wolf Mountains before daylight. It was a slow and difficult movement because of the terrain and the darkness, and after a ten mile march the column halted a little after 2:00 a.m., June 25, to await further word from the scouts. Lieutenant Edgerly said that the march resumed at 5:00 a.m., and that another halt was made "about 9:00 a.m. on the 25th," (other accounts say it was 8:00 a.m.) and that "General Custer, with Lieutenant Varnum and the scouts went to a neighboring hill to look at the village reported by the scouts to be visible from that point."[17]

The distance from the divide to the river is 13 miles and the village was an additional 2.2 miles north of that point. A line of sight estimate from the divide to the village would be a total of about 12 miles. However, the village was never visible from the divide because it was located along the west bank of the river which at that point was hidden by the long line of bluffs that border the river on the east bank. What the scouts saw was an indistinguishable mass of movement that they correctly believed was the pony herd. That information proved only that the hostiles were nearby, and Custer had to have more information than that. Neither he nor Varnum could see what the scouts had seen, even with binoculars, but they assumed the scouts were correct.

Lieutenant George Wallace, in his itinerary of the march, stated that "Custer determined to cross the divide that night (June 24), conceal the command, the next day find out the locality of the village, and attack the next morning (June 26) at daylight."[18] Again, circumstances beyond the control of the military forced a revision of those plans. Lieutenant Edgerly, after stating what Wallace had also said about Custer's plans, added, "While on this hill they were seen by six hostiles who were scouting near there. Our scouts made a dash for them but they escaped in the direction of the village."[19]

Custer's plan depended upon the premise that the troops would not be discovered, and the presence of the Indians on the divide, coupled with information Custer received when he returned to the command, strongly suggested that Custer's plan had been compromised. The latter incident, in Edgerly's account: Custer "was told by an officer that a Sergt. of Yates' troop who had been back on the trail a few miles to find some hard bread lost from a pack mule, had seen an Indian trying to break open the box. The officers were immediately assembled and General Custer said that of course all possibility of surprising the Indians was now gone and that the only way to catch them was to move on them at once. It was thought at that time that some of the Indians were already leaving, some officers imagining they saw quite a party moving off to the right of the village. General Custer then said that as soon as the troop commanders announced their troops mounted and ready to march he would assign them places, and that their positions in the advance would depend upon the order in which they reported."[20]

It was only a matter of moments before the troop commanders announced their readiness and the column prepared for action.

CHAPTER FOUR
"Reconnaissance in Force"

'When the Sioux and Cheyenne warriors returned to the main camp on Reno Creek, following the battle with Crook on the Rosebud, plans were made for the removal of the camp to a new location. Wooden Leg tells us that "all camps were moved again early the next morning," and the hostiles moved down Reno Creek a few miles, then turned south along the benchlands on the east side of the Little Big Horn. Again the Cheyennes were in the lead, the Uncpapas in the rear, and the other tribal units in between. After moving south toward the headwaters of the Little Big Horn, they made camp (marked "4" on the map on page 33).[1]

The Indians remained in this camp for six days, sending out hunting parties west of the river and grazing their ponies east of their camp. Wooden Leg emphasized that "our plans had been to go up the Little Bighorn valley. But our game scouts reported great herds of antelope west of the Bighorn river. Because of this the chiefs decided we should turn and go down the Little Bighorn, to its mouth. From there our hunting parties could cross the Bighorn and get antelope skins and meat that we now wanted."[2]

Consequently the Indians crossed the Little Big Horn and turned to the north, the Cheyennes in the lead, stopping after going about eight or nine miles, about two miles north of what was later the site of the Garryowen railroad station ("5" on the map).

Dr. Thomas Marquis estimated the number of Cheyennes present (based on Wooden Leg's data) at sixteen hundred, and the total of all the Indians at about twelve thousand. Other estimates have ranged up to nearly eighteen thousand with the warrior force between three and five thousand.[3]

It was June 24 when the village settled in its new camp, resting up for the move northward. That night there was dancing in the camps, partly as a delayed celebration of the victory over Crook. The dancing ended at dawn of June 25, and after a few hours sleep Wooden Leg and his brother Yellow Hair joined their friends who were bathing in the river. "The sun was high, the weather was hot," said Wooden Leg, and when they had finished bathing he and his brother sat under a tree and talked. "Before we knew it, both of us were sound asleep."[4]

The time was early afternoon, June 25.

One mile west of the divide, perhaps fifteen miles from where Wooden Leg and his brother lay sleeping, Custer made his battalion assignments. Sixteen of the regiment's officers were away on detached service or special duty, including Bvt. Maj. Gen. Samuel Sturgis, colonel of the regiment, and two of the majors, Col. Lewis Merrill and Lt. Col. Joseph Tilford. Four company commanders were also absent: Captain Owen Hale of "K" Co., Captain Charles Ilsley of "E," Bvt. Lt. Col. John Tourtellotte, captain of "G" Co., and Bvt. Lt. Col. Michael Sheridan (brother of General Phil Sheridan) captain of "L." Their commands were assigned to 1st Lieutenants Edward Godfrey, Algernon Smith, Donald McIntosh and James Calhoun, respectively. Five 1st lieutenants were absent and their functions were assigned to five of the eight 2nd lieutenants present, one of which was actually an infantry officer, pressed into service because of the shortage of officers.[5]

Col. Frederick Benteen, captain of Co. "H," was the first to report his company ready, and with his 1st Lieutenant, Frank Gibson, was given the advance. Custer assigned two other companies to Benteen: Co. "D," commanded by Bvt. Lt. Col. Thomas Weir and 2nd Lt. Winfield Scott Edgerly, and Co. "K," under 1st Lt. Edward S. Godfrey. Godfrey's 2nd lieutenant, Luther Hare, was detailed to assist Lt. Varnum with the scouts.

Benteen's orders were given to him by General Custer orally, and Benteen, in a letter to his wife on July 2, after the battle, described them briefly as follows: "I was ordered with three companies, D, H and K, to go to the left for the purpose of hunting for the valley of the river — Indian camp — or anything I could find."[6] In a later letter he said much the same thing: "I was ordered... to go over the immense hill to the left, in search of the valley, which was supposed to be very near by."[7]

Apparently other officers of his battalion were present when the orders were given and their versions generally agree with Benteen's. Edgerly recalled how the orders were given to Benteen by Custer: "Move off to the left (Custer indicating an angle of about 35 or 40 degrees from the direction of the village), attack any Indians you come across, and you will be supported."[8]

Lieutenant Gibson, Benteen's subordinate, said that his captain was "to take his battalion to the left... and if he found any Indians trying to escape up the valley of the Little Bighorn, to intercept them and drive them back in the direction the village was supposed to be... Should he find nothing he was to pick up the trail again and follow it on."[9]

From these versions — all basically in agreement — we are able to get some idea of how General Custer assessed the situation at that time. First, it is obvious that Custer did believe that in discovering the pony herd, the scouts had also discovered the general location of the Indians in the valley.

Second, by ordering Benteen's battalion to the left, Custer wanted to determine the *exact* location of the Indians. It was possible — indeed, based upon past experience, even probable — that the hostiles had encamped in separate tribal circles both north and south of the pony herd. If any were camped south of the herd, Benteen could easily ascertain this, and could possibly chase them north "so as to preclude the possibility of the escape of the Indians to the south or southeast by passing around your (Custer's) left flank," as General Terry had said in his letter of instructions to Custer. This was an important consideration, and before committing his troops to action, Custer must have this information. If no Indians were found to the south, Benteen was ordered to rejoin the regiment for a concerted attack upon the hostiles.

As Benteen's battalion moved out to the left, Custer continued with his assignments. Colonel Reno was given three companies: "A," commanded by Captain Myles Moylan and his 1st Lieutenant, Charles De Rudio. Moylan's 2nd Lieutenant, Charles Varnum, accompanied the battalion as Chief of Scouts, assisted by 2nd Lieutenant Luther Hare of Co. "K." Company "G" was commanded by 1st Lieutenant Donald McIntosh, whose 1st Lieutenant, George Wallace, also kept the itinerary. "M" Company was led by Captain Thomas French and 2nd Lieutenant Benjamin Hodgson of Co. "B," filling in for 1st Lt. Edward Mathey who was assigned to lead the packtrain escort.

In addition to the three companies, Reno was given two of the regiment's three medical officers: Assistant Surgeon Henry R. Porter and Acting Assistant Surgeon James De Wolf. The noted scout, Charley Reynolds, Interpreter Isaiah Dorman, George Herendeen (General Gibbon's scout), Fred Gerard, the Arickara Interpreter, two of the Crow scouts and about twenty Arickara scouts, including Bloody Knife, Custer's favorite, accompanied the Reno battalion.

Captain Thomas McDougall, commander of Co. "B," was assigned to guard the packtrain while Lt. Mathey led the escort made up of one non-commissioned officer and six privates from each company, except Co. "B." Eleven civilian packers led by John C. Wagoner, the Chief Packer, and Custer's personal orderly, John Burkman of Co. "L," accompanied the packtrain.

It is believed that the remaining five companies, "C," "E," "F," "I," and "L," were divided into two battalions, the first three companies commanded by Bvt. Lt. Col. George Yates, and the remaining two by Bvt. Lt. Col. Miles Keogh. However, there is no record of such a division and the five companies seem to have functioned as a single unit, probably under the direct command of General Custer. Company "C" was led by Bvt. Lt. Col. Thomas Custer, younger brother of the general, with his subaltern, 2nd Lt. Henry Harrington. "E" Company was commanded by Bvt. Captain Algernon Smith, 1st Lt. of Co. "A," and his 2nd Lt., James Sturgis. Col. Yates was captain of Co. "F," the "Band Box troop," assisted by 2nd Lt. William Van W. Reily. Col. Keogh commanded "I" Company, whose 1st Lieutenant was James Porter, and "L" Company was under the command of 1st Lt. James Calhoun, brother-in-law of the Custers, whose normal assignment was Co. "C." Calhoun was assisted by 2nd Lt. John J. Crittenden of the 20th Infantry.

The Headquarters staff consisted of General Custer, Bvt. Lt. Col. William Cooke, the Adjutant, Sergeant-Major William H. Sharrow and Chief Trumpeter Henry Voss. Also assigned to the staff were Sergeant Robert Hughes of "K" Company as Color Sergeant, and Private Henry Dose of "G" Company as Trumpeter. Corporal John Callahan of Co. "K" was assigned as hospital steward under Assistant Surgeon George E. Lord.[10]

In addition to the military personnel with the Custer

battalion were a number of civilians. Harry Armstrong Reed, nephew of the Custer brothers, was present as the guest of the General for the summer campaign; Mitch Bouyer, the half-Sioux Interpreter for the Crow Indians, accompanied the battalion as did Mark H. Kellogg, correspondent for the Bismarck (N.D.) *Tribune*, substituting for his editor, Col. C.A. Lounsberry who declined due to the illness of his wife. Boston Custer, youngest of the Custer brothers, who was carried on the rolls as a forage master, remained with the packtrain, but later joined his brother's battalion before it went into action.

The Benteen battalion started out with 116 men, including 5 officers. This total would later increase by one when Trumpeter Martin rejoined his company.

The Reno battalion started out with 168: 140 military personnel, 4 civilians, and 24 scouts. The battalion would lose two men sent as messengers before going into action: Privates Archibald McIlhargey and John Mitchell of Co. "I," whose bodies were found with their company.

The Custer battalion started with 217, including 13 officers, 197 enlisted men, 3 civilians and 4 scouts. Four men would be unable to keep up and would drop out of the battalion; two men would be sent as messengers (Martin and Kanipe), and two others (McIlhargey and Mitchell) would be received as messengers; one civilian would join later and 4 Crow scouts would be released before the battalion went into action. Actual battle strength of the three battalions was: Reno, 166; Benteen, 117; Custer, 210.[11]

Company "B," under the command of Captain McDougall, and the packtrain escorted by Lieutenant Mathey's contingent, started out with 121 enlisted men, 12 civilians and at least one Arickara scout, Pretty Face. As noted before Boston Custer later left the command and joined his brothers, leaving a total of 135 officers and enlisted men, civilians and scouts.

The regiment was now engaged in what Dr. Charles

RECONNAISSANCE IN FORCE 61

Kuhlman so aptly described as a "reconnaissance in force."[12] The exact location of the Indians had not yet been determined; that was the purpose of the regimental division into battalions, to reconnoiter the area and find the hostiles. Until that was done no plan of battle could be drawn up by Custer. So the troops moved out; Colonel Benteen's command was soon out of sight as they wended their way down a ravine to the left, and Colonel Reno's battalion moved to the south bank of Reno Creek. General Custer's five companies marched parallel to Reno on the north bank. About twenty minutes later the packtrain and escort followed and the march was on to the Little Big Horn.

Seven and a half miles from the point where the regiment was divided the south fork of Reno Creek joined the main stream, and here the troops found the site of what appeared to be a recently evacuated village.[13] At least one tepee was standing near the forks and in it was found the body of a warrior who had apparently died of wounds received in the fight against Crook at the big bend just seven days before. As the troops reached the campsite, Fred Gerard, a civilian interpreter, rode slightly ahead and to the right of the column to the top of a small hillock. From this vantage point he could see a cloud of dust and a number of mounted Indians riding hard downstream. Turning to Custer, Gerard shouted, "There go your Indians, General, running like devils!"[14]

It is now known that these Indians, perhaps forty or fifty in number, were a band of Cheyennes on their way to the main camp of the hostiles and that they veered off at the approach of the soldiers, not reaching the camp until after the battle. Custer, however, could not know this; he was on the trail of the hostiles and now they had been sighted, running away as Terry, Gibbon and Custer feared they would do at the approach of the troops. Gerard's assumption that the Indians he saw "running like devils" were the rear guard of the main body of hostiles desperately trying to escape made it necessary for Custer to commit the regiment to action prematurely. The "reconnaissance in force" was ended; Custer, believing he had contacted the enemy in flight, had no course open to him but to attack.

Quickly he ordered the Arikara scouts to pursue and harass the fleeting hostiles in order to slow them down, but the scouts refused to attack, assuming that Custer was sending them forward alone. Gerard explained to them that the soldiers would be with them and they rode forward. Custer then turned to his adjutant with orders for Reno to take up the pursuit. Cooke rode over to Reno and delivered the order: "The Indians are two miles and a half ahead; move forward as fast as you can and charge them as soon as you find them, and we will support!"[15]

Reno followed the scouts who were now about a half mile ahead toward the valley of the Little Big Horn.

Events following the division of the regiment can be placed in a time sequence, but only approximately. Lieutenant Wallace, who kept the itinerary, said that it was 12:05 p.m. (Chicago time) when the halt was made about a mile west of the divide where the battalion assignments were issued. The next time he looked at his watch, about one mile before reaching the forks of Reno Creek (the site of the Lone Tepee), it was 2:00 o'clock. However the distances can be determined quite accurately and this information can be correlated with the cavalry's official "table of equitation:" at a walk, the cavalry would cover a mile every 15 minutes (4 miles per hour); at a trot, one mile every 7½ minutes (8 m.p.h.); at a gallop, one mile every 5 minutes (12 m.p.h.), and at an extended gallop or "charge," one mile every 3 minutes and 45 seconds (16 m.p.h.).[16] These figures are much too precise, of course, but they do provide a basis for estimating the time it took to cover a known distance. The terrain is also a factor, but the ride down

Reno Creek was over fairly level ground with few obstructions since only a week earlier perhaps 12,000 Indians and as many horses had traveled this same route and would surely have cleared away most of the brush and deadwood.

The difficulties in making precise statements as to the time it took to arrive at a given point are further compounded by some disagreement among the participants as to the actual gait traveled, but these differences of opinion are not disparate enough to prevent us from making estimates that are reasonably approximate.

Using the data on hand we can determine that Reno and Custer started out about one mile west of the divide at 12:15 p.m. According to Wallace, they were one mile east of the Lone Tepee at 2:00 p.m., having covered a distance of 7½ miles. The gait must have been a fast walk, a little over 4 miles an hour. There was no reason for them to go faster than this, especially since Custer was allowing time for Benteen to complete his scout to the southwest and rejoin the regiment. No firm plans could be made until Custer knew whether there were Indians south of the pony herd.

The Lone Tepee was reached at 2:15 p.m., one mile at a walk, and as Gerard's sighting of the Cheyennes riding away in a cloud of dust took place as the troops reached the tepee, the pause there should have been brief — long enough for Custer's argument with the scouts and his subsequent order to Reno to continue the pursuit — probably no more than five minutes.

Reno had about four and a half miles to go to the river, trotting most of the way in order to save the horses for the charge once the Indians were sighted. The advance should have been accomplished in 30 minutes, which would bring Reno to the Little Big Horn at about 2:50 p.m.

Lieutenant Hare and Fred Gerard had ridden ahead with the scouts and after watering their horses, rode down the valley for about a mile, apparently to drive off the hostiles' pony herd. A small number of Sioux spotted them and came riding toward them. Gerard realized that the Indians were not running away as he had previously reported to Custer and he immediately rode back to the ford where Reno's troops were completing their crossing. From the river he saw Col. Cooke about a half mile east, riding back to join Custer. Gerard rode after him, overtaking him about a mile from the river.

"I told him that Reno and his battalion had forded and that the Indians were coming up the valley to meet him, and I thought the General ought to know that the Indians were showing fight instead of running away. He said: 'All right, Gerard, you go ahead, and I will go back and report.'"[17]

Gerard rode back at the gallop, returning in time to join Charley Reynolds at the rear of Reno's battalion as it was forming up to advance down the valley. The time was now 3:10 p.m.

Cooke had only a few hundred yards to go to reach the Custer battalion, now about a mile from the river. The information Cooke brought must have caused Custer some concern, and decided him to make a personal appraisal of the situation.[18] Ordering the command forward, he turned sharply to the north, stopping briefly at the north fork of Reno Creek to water the horses, then rode at an extended gallop to the bluffs bordering the east bank of the Little Big Horn. There, just north of what later was known as Reno Hill, Custer was able to see the valley below, and saw Reno's command charging up the plain, apparently without opposition. From this point on the bluffs Custer's view of the Indian encampment was obscured by the heavily timbered river. Custer had now traveled about two miles from the point where Cooke had met him, and at an extended gallop he would have covered that distance in about fifteen minutes, including the time spent watering the horses at the north fork. Sergeant Daniel Kanipe tells us that it was shortly after this that his captain, Lt. Col. Tom Custer, gave him the General's order to take a message to Captain McDougall.

"Go back to McDougall and bring him and the pack train straight across the country. Tell McDougall to hurry the pack train and if any of the packs get loose cut them and let them go; do not stop to tighten them. And if you see Benteen, tell him to come on quick — a big Indian camp."[19]

Turning north again, Custer rode another mile to the head of a coulee which begins about a quarter of a mile south of what is now called "Weir Point" and skirts this promontory on the east, emptying into Medicine Tail Coulee. A "tradition" has grown up in the historical reconstruction of the Custer Battle that the General, his brother Tom, his adjutant and Trumpeter Martin all rode to the top of the highest hill on Weir Point for a second observation. Here he is supposed to have exclaimed, "We've caught them napping!" and then to have sent Martin off with the famous order to Benteen, written by Cooke, the Adjutant: "Benteen. Come on. Big village. Be quick. Bring packs." Then the hurried signature, "W.W. Cooke," and a post-script: "P.S. Bring pacs *[sic]*."[20]

Actually, there is no evidence that Custer ever ascended Weir Point at all, and Martin, who told of only *one* observation of the valley by Custer, said that Custer and the battalion "rode on, pretty fast, until we came to a big ravine that led in the direction of the river, and the General pointed down there and then called me. This was about a mile down the river from where we went up on the hill."[21]

A mile from the observation point on the bluffs north of Reno Hill would bring the battalion to the head of Cedar Coulee, east of Weir Point, and Martin said it was at this place that he was given the message for Benteen.

Walter Camp, in his 1908 interview with Curly, the Crow scout who rode with the battalion at least to this point, was told that Custer passed along the bluffs for fully three-quarters of a mile in plain sight of Reno's men in the valley to Cedar Coulee. Camp, summarizing Curly's account, said: "Bouyer and his four scouts kept to the left [west] of Custer on the crest of the high ridge and peaks [Weir Point], and at all times could command a view of the river and the bottoms beyond. Before Bouyer got to the peaks, he left three of his Crow scouts behind, with orders to watch the Indian camp in the valley opposite and any movements of Indians in Custer's rear. Taking Curly with him, he passed on and over the peaks, and then on a course parallel with that of Custer [directly north] until they came down into the bed of [Medicine Tail Coulee], where they met Custer about one-half mile from the river. When they got to the top of the first of these peaks, they looked across and observed that Reno's command was fighting. At the sight of this, Bouyer could hardly restrain himself and shouted and waved his hat excitedly for some little time. Undoubtedly," Camp concluded, "Bouyer is the same man seen by some in Reno's command to wave his hat, for Custer never went to the peaks or high ridge; and when the hat was waved, Custer was entirely out of sight from Reno's position."[22] This account contradicts De Rudio's testimony that he recognized Custer as the one who waved his hat, and who said it was *not* on Weir Point, as will be developed in Chapter Five.

The Custer battalion continued down the coulee to the northeast as Martin rode off with his message for Benteen. He had gone only a short distance when he met Boston Custer, the youngest of the brothers, who asked, "Where's the General?"

Martin replied, "Right behind that next ridge you'll find him," and then continued on his way.[23]

It is more difficult to provide a time-frame for the Benteen battalion on their scout to the left, chiefly because their line of march is not known. However it is possible to make some conclusions on the basis of the known data when placed in relation to the movements of the packtrain.

Benteen said that he left the division point at 12:10 p.m. This would be about five minutes before Custer and Reno would set out, and the evidence does support this earlier departure. As Benteen led his troops out to the left, he passed Reno and told him where he was going. At the time of this brief conversation, Reno had not as yet received his own assignment.[24]

In order to calculate the times and distances involved in the Benteen scout, it is necessary to deal first with the packtrain, for we know its location at the time Benteen joined the main trail.

Captain McDougall and the packtrain left the division point some 20 or 30 minutes after the rest of the regiment. The departure time is usually estimated as 12:30 p.m. Although cavalry horses walked at the rate of four miles an hour, heavily-laden mules would obviously move at a slower pace. All along the march to this point the mules had caused numerous delays, a situation which must have continued on their trek down Reno Creek.

About three miles from the division point (four miles from the Camp Marker on the divide), a spring feeding into Reno Creek had saturated the surrounding area and created what was called "the morass." The location of this boggy area by Pvt. John Burkman makes it possible for us to determine the extent of Benteen's scout to the southwest.[25]

Lieutenant Edgerly tells us that "Benteen moved in the direction ordered until we came to some steep and high hills, where he ordered Lt. Gibson to ride to the top of them and see if there were any Indians in sight. Gibson reporting to the negative, the battalion skirted the hills looking for a chance to break through the chain without giving the horses and men a too-fatiguing climb. This, of course, brought us to the right and nearly parallel with Reno's trail, *in less than an hour.* [Italics mine, CdB.] About this time Mr. Boston Custer, the General's youngest brother, rode by on his pony. He had stayed back with the pack train and was now hurrying up to join the General's immediate command. He gave me a cheery salutation as he passed and then, with a smile on his face, rode to his death..."[26]

As Benteen's battalion joined the main trail along Reno Creek they saw the packtrain approaching about a half mile east, and after following the trail for another mile they came to the morass. According to Benteen they reached the morass at 1:30.[27]

When Benteen joined the trail the packtrain was still a mile and a half from the morass, and was then half-way between the division point and the spring.[28] They reached the morass at 2:00 p.m. as Benteen was leaving it, which means they had traveled only at the rate of 2 miles per hour (3 miles in 90 minutes). The time Benteen joined the main trail, ending his scout, was then 1:15 p.m. Fifteen minutes later he was at the morass (1 mile at 4 m.p.h.). Benteen had been on his scout for only one hour and five minutes (12:10 to 1:15 p.m.). At 4 miles an hour he could not have covered more than a fraction over four miles — two miles longer than if he had come straight down from the division point! This attests to the accuracy of Edgerly's statement that the scout had taken one hour, and Benteen's own admission that he reached the morass at 1:30. The total mileage of the scout is considerably less than the "10 to 15" mile total estimated by some of the officers,[29] and Benteen could not have been more than a mile south of the main trail at his farthest point, which explains the statements made later by Benteen and also Lt. Godfrey that on their march they had occasional glimpses of the Custer battalion's "Grey Horse" troop (Company "E").[30]

Benteen spent a half hour at the morass watering the command's horses, a delay that caused some uneasiness among his officers.[31] Finally, Colonel Weir started off with his company and the rest of the battalion followed, just as the lead

RECONNAISSANCE IN FORCE   69

mules of the packtrain, catching the scent of water, rushed into the muddy morass.

As Benteen set out from the watering-place, Custer and Reno were only three and a half miles ahead of him, one mile from the Lone Tepee. Had Benteen not loitered so long at the morass he would have been even closer, for Reno and Custer would have passed that point at about 1:00 p.m., a half hour before Benteen reached it.

The 4½ mile ride from the morass to the Lone Tepee would take one hour and fifteen minutes at a walk, which according to Edgerly, was the pace. Passing the tepee at 3:15 p.m., Benteen proceeded at least a mile further west, and at about 3:40 p.m. Sergeant Kanipe rode by with his message for the packtrain commander. As Kanipe passed Benteen he said, "they want you up there as quick as you can get there — they have struck a big Indian camp."[32] A mile further Private Martin rode up and handed Benteen the order from Custer. Benteen read it, showed it to Weir, Edgerly and perhaps some others, then proceeded on at a trot. It was now about 3:50 p.m.

CHAPTER FIVE
"The Valley Fight"

At approximately 3:10 p.m., Reno, with "A" and "M" Companies in line and "G" Company in reserve, prepared to advance down the broad, flat plain that characterizes this part of the Little Big Horn valley, the scouts ahead and to the left of the battalion. Sgt. Stanislas Roy, a Frenchman who had served with the 7th Cavalry since 1869, said that he heard some of the men say "There goes Custer" while the command was still forming up after the crossing.[1] As the battalion moved down the valley at a brisk trot, Pvt. Thomas O'Neill recalled that he, too, saw the Custer battalion on the bluffs east of the river.[2]

Pvt. Henry Petring, riding with his company, "G" in the rear of the line, said, "While in the bottom, going toward the skirmish line, I saw Custer over across the river on the bluffs, waving his hat. Some of the men said: 'There goes Custer. He is up to something, for he is waving his hat.'"[3] Lt. DeRudio, who also saw this incident, places it much later in the action.[4]

As the command drew closer to the "Garry Owen" loop of the river, "G" Company was called up into line on the right and the pace increased to a gallop. A few mounted warriors, probably all Uncpapa Sioux, could be seen ahead of them, and through the dust the troopers could see a few of the Uncpapa tepees extending out a little past the loop of the river which effectively hid the larger part of the encampment. About a thousand yards from the village Reno suddenly ordered the command to halt, and the troopers were thrown into a dismounted skirmish line with each fourth man dropping back to hold the horses of the three men ahead of him and moving them to the right to be sheltered in the timber bordering the river.

Pvt. Roman Rutten of Co. "M" had been experiencing difficulty with his horse since the charge began, and when the command to halt was given, Rutten's horse "lunged ahead of the command and took him considerably nearer the Indians. He therefore circled him around to the right, and came back through the timber and joined the command."[5] Privates John H. Meier, Henry Turley and George E. Smith, all of "M" Company, had the same problem with their excited horses. Meier, wounded in the neck, and Turley, who would later be killed, made it back to their unit, but Smith could not control his horse and rode on into the village to certain death.[6]

About the time the halt was ordered, First Sgt. William Heyn of Co. "A" was wounded in the knee, and a few minutes later Sgt. Miles O'Hara of Co. "M" was wounded on the skirmish line.[7] After dismounting, the line moved forward a few yards and the Indians whose numbers were increasing steadily, began to work toward them, apparently emboldened by the weakness of the line, now depleted by the detached horseholders and the few casualties. Nine officers, four civilians, a few scouts and less than a hundred enlisted men formed the skirmish line and as more warriors came forward it became obvious that the left flank of the line was in danger of collapse.

It was about 3:20 p.m. when the skirmish line was formed, and the fighting there continued only about fifteen minutes. At approximately 3:35 the troops were ordered to fall back into the timber along the west bank of the stream and here they found an excellent defensive position in a dry river bed, the current of the river having rechanneled itself further east,

THE VALLEY FIGHT 73

leaving a dry cutbank about four feet lower than the plain. Protected by the riverbank itself, and the brush that hid the soldiers from the view of the hostiles, the troops were able to see the Indians on the plain in front of them and most of the Indian casualties probably took place during this part of the fighting.

The command quickly spread through the woods in all directions to prevent the hostiles from infiltrating. There were no further casualties at this time although Lt. De Rudio had apparently brought in Sgt. Charles White of Co. "M" who had been wounded on the skirmish line.[8] There is no evidence that anything was done to rescue Sgt. O'Hara, also wounded on the line, but he probably died before the move to the timber was made. His body was found about 40 or 50 yards from the timber.[9]

Wooden Leg and his brother, fast asleep on the river bank at the north end of the village, were awakened by gunshots. "The shooting was somewhere at the upper part of the camp circles," he recalled. "It looked as if all the Indians there were running away toward the hills to the westward or down toward our end of the village. Women were screaming and men were letting out war cries. Through it all we could hear old men calling: 'Soldiers are here! Young men, go out and fight them.'"[10]

Wooden Leg's father had caught his son's horse when it was brought in with others by the boys who were acting as horseherders. The young Cheyenne made hasty ceremonial preparations for battle, then mounting his pony he rode with a few others through the village toward the sound of battle. As they neared the Uncpapa circle they "saw many hundreds of Indians on horseback... dashing to and fro in front of a body of soldiers on the level valley ground shooting with rifles."[11] It was Reno's skirmish line, and only a moment later the line moved into the timber.

In the timber there was little activity. "G" Company was

ordered to move to the river on the east side of the loop to watch for possible infiltration by the Indians whose numbers continued to increase. Just how many warriors Reno was facing is not known, and estimates made by the survivors varied considerably, from Dr. Porter's guess of 200-300 to Col. Reno's estimate of 600-900. The truth is probably somewhere in between — perhaps as many as 500 Indians had gathered around the timber, but with no visible targets there was little for them to do but to fire into the woods in the hope of hitting a soldier. Wooden Leg said that "Arrows were showered in to the timber. Bullets whistled out toward the Sioux and Cheyennes. But we stayed far back while we extended our curved line farther and farther around the big grove of trees."[12]

There is no doubt that Reno disobeyed his orders to charge the Indians when he halted his command a thousand yards from the nearest tepees, but whether he could have forced his way through the village successfully is still a matter of controversy. In his Official Report Reno described his actions: "I deployed, and with the Ree scouts on my left, charged down the valley, driving the Indians with great ease for about 2½ miles. I, however, soon saw that I was being drawn into some trap, as they certainly would fight harder, and especially as we were nearing the village, which was still standing; besides, I could not see Custer or any other support; and at the same time the very earth seemed to grow Indians, and they were running toward me in swarms, and from all directions. I saw I must defend myself and give up the attack mounted."

Lt. Edgerly, who was not with the Reno battalion, commented on this passage: "The few warriors who opposed Reno were so demoralized that they offered but a feeble resistance, thus causing him to believe he was being drawn into ambush, and to halt near the village till the arrival of the mounted warriors..."

He concluded, "What would have happened if Reno had

charged through the village as we found it, is a matter of conjecture. I believe that we would have captured and destroyed the village and won a costly victory."[13]

Lt. Hare, who *was* present, when asked about the number of Indians opposing Reno's charge, replied, "If there were any, they were very few."[14] George Herendeen was asked the same question. His answer: "I did not see any and I was in front. The Indians were sitting still on their horses, seemed to be awaiting our approach, and did not move till we got near where the command dismounted."[15]

Other officers present supported Reno's decision, including Lt. Hare, who said that if the command had continued for another three hundred yards, they would not have survived five minutes, a statement which is difficult to reconcile with his previous assertion. Lt. De Rudio said that the command would have been destroyed had they continued five hundred yards further.[16]

Reno's decision to halt the charge and form a skirmish line was a judgment call, one which a commander must be expected to make on the basis of his assessment of the situation, and whether it was a wise decision or a tactical error could not be known at the time it was made. This is the kind of dilemma faced by military leaders in circumstances that demand an instant determination of what course must be followed, and will inevitably be subject to the scrutiny of hindsight.

The wisdom of Reno's next decision, however, is not debatable; it flew in the face of accepted military strategy and discipline, it cost the lives of thirty-seven more members of his battalion, and it effectively sealed the fate of Custer and those who rode with him.

Reno had apparently established his command post in a clearing near the center of the timber. Surrounded by some members of troops "A" and "M" and the medical staff's improvised hospital, he suddenly decided to abandon his highly defensible position in the woods, and ordered the men to mount their horses. Those immediately around him heard the order and hastened to comply with it, but as soon as they swung into their saddles they were raised above the shelter of the cutbank and presented the Indians with a visible target. A number of shots were fired at them by the hostiles and Pvt. Klotzbucher, mounted next to Reno, fell mortally wounded, crying, "Oh my God. I've got it!" Custer's favorite Arickara scout, Bloody Knife, mounted in front of Reno and was killed instantly by a bullet which exploded his head, his blood and brains splattering over Reno who quickly countermanded his own order and shouted, "Dismount!" He had no more than struck the ground when he changed his mind again and once more ordered the men to mount. Then, turning his horse he rode out of the timber onto the plain, followed by those who had heard the order.

Sgt. Roy of "A" Company said to Lt. Wallace, "Lieutenant, I cannot find my horse." Men from his company and also from Company "M" had already ridden out and Wallace replied, "Take any horse you can find and get out of here quick, or get on a horse behind someone. Get out any way you can..."[17]

Roy said he saw Pvt. John Gilbert of his company leading four horses out of the timber and Roy recognized one of them as his. "I mounted up and followed the column and yelled to Gilbert to follow the column and 'git.' I was behind Gilbert and very late in getting out of the timber. About 75 or 100 yards from the timber I saw Charlie Reynolds dismounted and wounded, with a pistol, standing still and showing fight. Soon after this my horse was shot through the jaws just back of the mouth." The horse went down, Roy's sling belt flew over his head and his carbine went with it. Fortunately, both horse and rider got up again and Roy, armed only with a pistol, rode on.[18]

Pvt. Rutten of Company "M" said that as the men were

mounting up he heard his 1st Sergeant, James Ryan, ask Capt. French where they were going, and before French could answer, Reno rode past them shouting, "Everybody follow me."[19]

The Indians were caught by surprise; Wooden Leg described the movement from the perspective of the hostiles: "Suddenly the hidden soldiers came tearing out on horseback, from the woods. I was around on the side when they came out. I whirled my horse and lashed it into a dash to escape from them. All others of my companions did the same. But soon we discovered they were not following us. They were running away from us. They were going as fast as their tired horses could carry them across an open valley space and toward the river. We stopped, looked a moment, and then we whipped our ponies into swift pursuit. A great throng of Sioux also were coming after them. My distant position put me among the leaders in the chase. The soldier horses moved slowly, as if they were very tired. Ours were lively. We gained rapidly on them."[20]

Shortly after leaving the timber Rutten saw Isaiah Dorman's horse go down, and Dorman, dropping to one knee, continued to fire his rifle at the Indians. "Isaiah and I were intimate acquaintances, and as I passed him he looked up at me and cried out, 'Goodbye Rutten.' Cpl. Scollin fell in some low or soggy ground not far from the timber, and beyond this some distance was Lt. McIntosh trying to make his way. He was singled out by himself, and he was trying to urge his horse along but was not succeeding well. His lariat was dragging, which seemed to bother the horse. McIntosh was surrounded by twenty or thirty Indians, who were circling about him, apparently determined to get him."[21]

Pvt. Petring of Co. "G" found his horse had been killed in the timber and he took the horse of Pvt. Eldorado Robb. "As I emerged from the timber onto open ground, this horse was shot from under me. I ran back into the timber and saw a few horses running around loose and caught one of them up. My company had now been gone some time and in the confusion, I could not satisfy myself which direction they went," he said, but he rode on toward the river.[22]

Sergeant Thomas O'Neill's horse was shot as he was trying to mount it. Finding another horse nearby he mounted and started to ride out when he was stopped by Cpl. James Martin who claimed the horse was his. O'Neill relinquished the horse, and Martin rode out to his death. O'Neill and some others who were dismounted tried to follow the column on foot, but were fired upon by Indians and forced to run back to the timber, one of the men being killed before he reached the woods.[23]

Back in the timber, unable to join their retreating comrades, were Lt. De Rudio, the wounded Sgt. White, Pvts. O'Neill, McCormick, Korn, Sievertson and others, including the civilians, Herendeen and Gerard. By this time it is probable that Pvts. Klotzbucher and Lorentz had died of their wounds. It is reported that seventeen men were left behind in the timber, most of them eventually rejoining the troops on the bluffs.

The retreat started in panic and ended in chaos; it was, in Capt. French's words, a "sauve qui peut movement," ("save himself who can"). The troopers were strung out from the timber to the river, three-quarters of a mile away. All along the route, the hostiles, recovering from their surprise at the movement, began to ride alongside the fleeing troopers, clubbing them from their saddles.

"Indians mobbed the soldiers floundering afoot and on horseback in crossing the river," Wooden Leg said. "I do not know how many of our enemies might have been killed there. With my captured rifle as a club I knocked two of them from their horses into the flood waters. Most of the pursuing warriors stopped at the river, but many kept on after the men with the blue clothing. I remained in the pursuit and crossed the river."[24]

At the river, some of the lead horses balked at the steep bank and were forced into the stream from the pressure of those behind them. No attempt was made to provide covering fire for the men as they struggled through the water, and by a supreme effort succeeded in climbing out again on the east side of the stream.

"When I reached the river," said Rutten, "the water ahead of me was full of horses and men struggling to get across. I thought I had better keep out of the muddle and so turned my horse downstream. The opposite bank was high and steep, and men were riding both upstream and downstream trying to find some place to get up. Finally the mob of horsemen made for a narrow trail cut by buffalo in going for water, which cut through the steep bank at a moderate incline." It was, he said, "a hard test of horse flesh."[25]

Some of the men were unable to make it across with the lead group. Pvt. Henry Petring of "G" Company got part of the way, but saw a group of Indians on the opposite bank. "One Indian, on a cream colored pony, drew up his gun as if to fire, and I, knowing that I was in great danger and would have to act quickly, drew up my carbine without taking aim and fired, and both the pony and the Indian dropped. Then I, in order to get away quickly, jumped down off my horse and started downstream as fast as I could in water waist deep and deeper." Eventually Petring reached cover under some willows and there he found Pvt. Benjamin Johnson, also of "G" Company. "We got together, and soon one after another began to come along, and we soon had quite a party — a dozen or more dismounted men," including the wounded Sergeant White. About sundown, they were able to make their way across the river and "we all went up the bluffs together and joined Reno's command on the hill."[26]

Not all of them made it, of course. Lt. Benjamin Hodgson was struck in the hip or leg by a bullet which also killed his horse. Catching the stirrup of Trumpeter Charles Fischer of

Company "M," he was dragged across the river, but as he began his ascent of the bluffs he was shot again and killed. Dr. James De Wolf and his orderly tried to climb by way of a ravine to the left and both were killed by Indians who were above them on the bluffs.

Those troops following Reno made their way up a ravine to the right of that chosen by De Wolf and after reaching the hilltop, they moved about five hundred yards south to what is now known as Reno Hill. Had any significant number of Indians pursued the soldiers to the bluffs there is little doubt that the command would have been annihilated. Those that had ascended ahead of the soldiers, Wooden Leg included, remained some distance north, firing an occasional rifle shot in the direction of the troops. A short time later the fighting ended in the valley; most of the soldiers in the open near the river were killed, and those in and near the timber remained there in concealment, abandoning their attempt to escape.

When it was over, thirty-nine men lay dead in the valley, including three officers, thirty-one enlisted men, two civilians and three Indian scouts.

Perhaps the most telling comment on Reno's wild retreat was voiced by the Cheyennes: "We could never understand why the soldiers left the timber, for if they had stayed there the Indians could not have killed them."[27]

CHAPTER SIX
"The Battle on the Bluffs"

As Benteen's battalion neared the river, firing could be heard ahead and to the right. The command drew pistols and proceeded at the gallop. To the north they saw a group of soldiers atop the bluffs and others below in the valley still trying to reach the river. Benteen drew within two hundred yards of Reno's position before he was seen, and Reno ran out to meet him. "For God's sake, Benteen," he shouted, "halt your command and help me! I've lost half my men!"

Quickly the reinforcements moved into the hill position. It was now, according to Lt. Godfrey, 4:20 p.m.[1] Nearly all the testimony agrees that Benteen arrived ten minutes after Reno reached the hill, which makes it possible for us to determine how long the troops had been in the valley. As stated previously, fighting on the skirmish line, starting at approximately 3:20 p.m., lasted about fifteen minutes. The move to the timber at 3:35 p.m. would leave thirty-five minutes for both the fight there and the subsequent retreat, Reno having reached the bluffs at 4:10 p.m. The retreat must have started at least fifteen minutes before 4:10 p.m. It was three-quarters of a mile from the timber position to the place the command struck the river, and that distance could have been covered by the vanguard in five minutes. Crossing the stream under fire and ascending the steep bluffs would have taken at least another ten minutes, and perhaps even more for those in the rear of the column. It would seem reasonable, then, to conclude that the fight in the timber lasted no more than 20 minutes, and probably less: from 3:35 to 3:55 p.m.

The approach of Benteen had been seen by the hostiles and they broke off the engagement, leaving only a small number of snipers to harass the troops on the hill with an occasional rifle shot.[2] For Reno's men it was a welcome respite, and for the Benteen battalion it was an opportunity to bring some order to the situation by helping the survivors to recover from their frightening ordeal.

About ten minutes after Benteen's arrival Reno ordered Lt. Hare to find the packtrain and bring it up. Hare left at approximately 4:30 and found Captain McDougall's command about a mile east of Reno Hill.[3]

"Then came a time of suspense," said Lt. Edgerly. "We could hear heavy firing down the river and knew it must be Custer. "D" Company [Weir's] was for a long time standing to horse, every man apparently anxious to move down to the firing. I wondered what we were waiting for and said to Captain Weir, 'We ought to go down there.' Weir went away for a few minutes then came back again and asked me what I thought we ought to do. I replied, 'Go to Custer, of course.'

"He then asked if I would be willing to go with him and D troop, even if the other troops did not go. I told him I would and he then left me saying that he would ask permission of Reno and Benteen. Before reaching these officers, however, he changed his mind and concluded that before asking permission to take the troop down he would go to a high point that overlooked the valley and see what was going on there, so he came back toward the troop, called to an orderly to bring his horse, mounted and started toward the Custer battle ground, without saying a word to me. I, supposing from our conversa-

THE BATTLE ON THE BLUFFS 83

tion and his action, that he had received the desired permission, mounted the troop and started after him."[4]

It was about 4:40 p.m. when "D" Company set out, and Lt. Hare, returning ten minutes later from his ride to the packtrain, saw them perhaps three-quarters of a mile away.[5] Reno had appointed Hare as his acting adjutant, replacing the fallen Lt. Hodgson, and now ordered Hare to go after Weir and tell him to open communications with Custer. Hare rode off and joined "D" Company which had by this time reached the high promontories now called "Weir Point," about a mile and a half north.

The packtrain had obviously been following Custer's trail, not Reno's, for Hare found them north of the North Fork of Reno Creek, and when Hare diverted them to Reno's position on the hill, McDougall, heading north, had to turn left to the west.[6]

Captain McDougall reached the hill occupied by Reno and Benteen at 4:50 p.m., although the rest of the packtrain escorted by Lt. Mathey did not arrive until about an hour later. McDougall said that "all was quiet" when he got there, and that "one would not have imagined that a battle had been fought." Noting that no defense perimeter had been established, McDougall took it upon himself to form his company on a skirmish line, knowing that if the Indians were to attack at this time they could easily annihilate the seven companies on the hill.[7]

Firing from the north which had begun shortly after Hare left for the packtrain could still be heard, and there was much comment among the men and officers about it, including a remark by Lt. Godfrey that "the command ought to do something or Custer will be after Reno with a big stick."[8] McDougall, too, was concerned and told Godfrey, "I think we ought to go down there with him."[9] Nothing was done, however, and though most of the men later testified to the firing, Reno and Benteen both denied hearing it.

It is difficult to understand the obvious dawdling of the battalion commanders on the hill. Reno, the ranking officer, should certainly have accepted the responsibility of command and moved the regiment to the sound of the guns. Failing that, Benteen as senior captain, realizing Reno's indolence, should have insisted that a relief column be sent. If Reno had then refused, Benteen should have detached his battalion and moved forward on his own authority. He was, after all, still under the direct, written order of Custer to "Come on — be quick — big village — bring packs," and only Custer could rescind that order.[10] Reno's excuse, that his battalion was out of ammunition and must wait for the packs to arrive, is suspect. Lt. Wallace said that when the ammunition arrived, only one box was opened, and one of the civilian packers testified that the ammunition boxes were not even opened until after the return of the troops from Weir Point.[11] It was a clear case of "coffee cooling," a phrase which Benteen himself used disparagingly to describe indolence on another — and unrelated occasion.

According to McDougall it was an hour and a half after he arrived on Reno Hill that the command finally moved out to join Weir's troop on Weir Point, which would be about 6:20 p.m.[12] Lt. Varnum, who thought the packs arrived twenty minutes after Benteen joined Reno (which would be 4:40 p.m.), said the command moved to Weir Point an hour and a half after this (6:10 p.m.).[13] By "splitting the difference," we can arrive at a figure of 6:15 p.m. Benteen led the advance with French's company, followed by Companies "K," "H," and finally, "A," who brought the wounded, probably assisted by the remnant of "G" Company and McDougall's Company "B."

Lt. Edgerly, who had taken the advance with his captain, Col. Weir, said that "Weir rode along the crest of the bluffs where Custer was last seen alive by many of our command and I took the troop a little to the right following a shallow ravine." Some Indians were sighted ahead, and Weir "from his high point saw them start and signalled for me to move to the right, continuing his signals until he had swung the troop completely around and brought it to where he was."[14] Edgerly claimed that the Indians seen to the north were "a large number," but this is obviously an exaggeration as no engagement with the hostiles took place until much later.

Weir Point is the name given to a high, triangular ridge a mile and a half northwest of Reno Hill, and three miles southeast of the monument on Custer Hill. It is distinguished by two prominent rounded hills (or knolls) atop the west end of the ridge, connected by a saddleback, and one hill east of the southernmost hill, also connected by a saddleback, but one which is not so obvious today having been cut down by the construction of the road connecting the two battlefields.

The ravine which Edgerly said he followed to the right of the ridges is today known as "Cedar Coulee," and it starts about a quarter of a mile south of Weir Point. As the other troops came up, they apparently fell in behind Company "D" which Edgerly had moved out of the ravine and onto the "peaks." Benteen, who had come up with Co. "M" rather than his own company, was apparently just south of Company "D." He said that when he arrived he "got the guidon of my own troop and jammed it down in a pile of stones which were on the high point, thinking perhaps the fluttering of same might attract attention from Custer's command if any were in close proximity. Reno had then got up to the point where I was."[15]

If the guidon incident is true, and there is no reason to doubt it, Benteen, later joined by Reno, were at the front of the troops on Weir Point. However, Lt. Hare stated that Reno and Benteen were standing about a half mile in the rear of Co. "D," and Capt. McDougall, in the rear of the column and therefore in the lead during the retreat back to Reno Hill, said that Benteen was with him.[16]

Lt. Wallace said that he saw several thousand Indians all over the Custer battlefield, riding around but not firing. Lt. Godfrey reported that Custer's battleridge and the area surrounding it was visible, but that he saw no Indians, no bodies — no fighting at the time. Lt. Hare, while out in advance with Company "D," disagreed. He said the Indians were thick over the Custer ridge and were firing, and at that moment, Hare thought Custer was fighting them. Benteen, of course, insisted that the battleridge was not even visible and said he saw no sign of troops or fighting anywhere.

Lt. Edgerly, in his narrative, said "We stayed out there about two hours according to my recollection, doing considerable shooting but I imagine very little hitting." This is certainly understandable; the small number of Indians facing the troops had excellent cover and were content to engage in an unaggressive sniping action, hoping to discourage the troops from advancing. The main body of the warriors were still busily engaged three miles away.

The "two hours" spent on Weir Point must have referred only to Edgerly's company, which arrived there a few minutes after 5:00 o'clock. The other troops could not have reached Weir Point before 6:30 p.m., which means they spent only a half hour at Weir Point. During the time they held the position there, firing continued from the north, ending shortly after the Reno-Benteen forces began their retreat.

Edgerly said that Weir left about an hour before the retreat began and went to Reno. "Near the close of the two hours, Capt. French, who was holding a crest very close to mine, called out to me, 'Edgerly! Major Reno has given orders for us to fall back.' I looked to the rear and saw H and K troops moving off — the former at a gallop and the latter dismounted. I told Capt. French that I had received no orders to go back, and in a few minutes he called to me again saying he had received orders and was going back. He then mounted his troop and galloped off."[17]

Who ordered the retreat? Reno later said that Lt. Hare, acting on his own, but using Reno's name, ordered the withdrawal, but Hare said emphatically that he "did no such thing."[18] Edgerly said that when he was ordered back there were not many Indians in his front and he obeyed reluctantly, and Godfrey said he was surprised when Hare rode up saying that Reno had ordered the troops to fall back. Benteen's second in command, Lt. Gibson, reported that Benteen said, "This is a hell of a place to fight Indians. I am going to see Reno and propose that we go back to where we lay before starting out here," referring to Reno hill.[19] Hare substantiates this, saying that when Benteen and Reno were standing a half mile back of Company "D," "Benteen suggested to Reno that they fall back as they were in a poor place for defense."[20]

Quite soon after the battle, both Reno and Benteen began to create the impression that the troops were forced to retreat by the Indians. In statements made to The New York *Herald*, August 8, 1876, Benteen told of "a company sent forward in the direction supposed to have been taken by Custer. After proceeding about a mile they were attacked and driven back."[21]

Reno, not to be outdone, said "the whole command moved forward, proceeding about a mile and a half. During this time chopping shots were heard. So numerous were the masses of Indians encountered that the command was obliged to dismount and fight on foot, retiring to the point which had first been selected."[22]

The retreat very nearly got out of hand; Company "M", who had not forgotten the terror of the ride from the timber to the river, left immediately at the gallop. Lt. Edgerly, seeing his own troop follow "M" Company at a gallop, shouted, "Bring those horses down to a trot!" and added that he was "actually thrilled with pride at the promptness and accuracy with which the order was obeyed."[23]

It was after 7:00 p.m. when the troops left the Weir ridges, and as the command wended its way back along the trail to Reno Hill, the Indians came over the ridges after them. Pvt. Vincent Charley, Farrier of "D" Company, was shot in the hip, and as he fell from his horse he struck his head upon a stone which caused some bleeding. Edgerly told him to take refuge in a nearby ravine and promised to come back for him, but was never able to do so. After the battle, Charley's body was found with a stick rammed down his throat.[24]

Lt. Godfrey, whose company was apparently bringing up the rear, saw that the number of the Indians was increasing. About 500 yards from Reno Hill, Godfrey halted his men. "I at once made up my mind that such a retreat and close pursuit would throw the whole command into confusion, and perhaps, prove disastrous. I dismounted my men to fight on foot, deploying as rapidly as possible without waiting for the formation laid down in tactics. Lt. Hare expressed his intention of staying with me 'Adjutant or no Adjutant.' The led horses were sent to the main command. Our fire in a short time compelled the Indians to halt and take cover, but before this was accomplished a second order came for me to fall back as quickly as possible to the main command."

Godfrey continued his holding action, moving back slowly, until all the other troops were on the hill. As the company reached the approach to Reno's position Godfrey "again drove the Indians to cover, and ordered the men to run to the lines," a movement which Godfrey said was executed "without a single casualty."[25]

It was about 7:30 p.m. when the last of the troops reached Reno Hill, and they were immediately assigned defensive positions along the perimeter of the hill. We get some idea of the scene in Benteen's words. "We had time sufficient to get some kind of a line formed: the first officer I saw when establishing a line, was Lt. Geo. D. Wallace. I said, Wallace, put the right of your troop here. His answer was, 'I have no troop, only three men.' Well, said I, stay here with your three men, and don't let them get away, I will have you looked out for: — and Wallace and the three men stayed, and they were looked out for. Col. Reno was on the left — forming the same line — which wasn't a line but an arc of a circle, rather irregularly described too. And when we met about centre, my own Troop remained to be disposed of, so I put it over much ground, almost as much as the other six companies occupied, protecting left flank, and well to the rear, just on the edge of line of bluffs, near river.

"The formation as described, was dismounted; the horses of command, being placed in a saucer like depression of prairie, the lower rim of the saucer, instead of a rim was a gentle slope. The hospital was established at the upper rim, and was about as safe a place as there was around the vicinity, the blue canopy of heaven being the covering."[26]

The hill was not the highest position in the area, and the Indians quickly gained the heights of what is now called "Sharpshooters' Hill," from which they poured a heavy concentration of fire upon the men below. Before darkness ended the seige, 1st Sgt. DeWitt Winney and Pvt. Julius Helmer, both of Company "K," were killed, and Sgt. George King of Company "A" was mortally wounded.[27] There were probably other casualties, but there is no specific mention of them by name. Sgt. Ryan gives us a description of the battle on the hill that evening: "The company on the right of my company had a number of men killed in a few minutes. There was a high ridge on the right and an opening on the right of our lines, and one Indian in particular I must give credit for being a good shot.

"While we were lying in this line he fired a shot and killed the fourth man on my right. Soon afterward he fired again and shot the third man. His third shot wounded the man on my right, who jumped back from the line, and down among the rest of the wounded. I thought my turn was coming next. I jumped up, with Capt. French, and some half a dozen members of my company, and, instead of firing straight to the front, as we had been doing up to the time of this incident, we wheeled to our right and put in a deadly volley, and I think we put an end to that Indian, as there were no more men killed at that particular spot."

"When dark set in," Ryan continued, "it closed the engagement on the twenty-fifth. We went to work with what tools we had, consisting of two spades, our knives and tin cups, and, in fact, we used pieces of hard tack boxes for spades, and commenced throwing up temporary works. We also formed breastworks from boxes of hard bread, sacks of bacon, sacks of corn and oats, blankets, and in fact everything that we could get hold of.

"During the night ammunition and the rations reached us where we were entrenched in the lines, but we suffered severely from lack of water. Although the river was only three or four hundred yards away, we were unable to get any water, as the Indians held the approach to it. During the night several men made attempts to get water, but they were killed or driven back."[28]

Finally, all possible fortifications having been made, the troops relaxed, some of them, Edgerly tells us, "smoking their pipes and talking over the events of the day and the probabilities for the morrow, and some sleeping as soundly and snoring as loudly as if they were in their bunks in garrison."[29]

As the first faint streaks of dawn lighted the Montana sky, the troops on the hill were wakened. Lt. Gibson said that the trumpeters were ordered to sound reveille at daybreak "so as to notify all concerned, including the Indians, that there were still some men left on the hill."[30] Suddenly, two shots rang out, followed by a fusillade from every direction and the battle was on again.

Benteen's Company "H" occupied the southernmost extension of the hill, a position that afforded the least protection from the hostile fire, for the men — facing south — were especially vulnerable to the sharpshooters on the higher ridges in back of them, as well as those in the ravine on their front. The fault was Benteen's own; he was the only troop commander who had failed to order his men to fortify their positions, a situation which he tried to remedy only after a number of his men were killed or wounded.[31] Pvt. Rutten of Company "M" said that Benteen came to Reno asking for reinforcements, stating that he was "rapidly losing his men and that if he did not get assistance soon, he could not hold his hill."[32] Reno told him to take one of the other companies and Benteen chose French's troop, "M," whose blacksmith, Walter O. Taylor, said, "As for H Troop I know that during the forenoon of the 26th, I with others was ordered to take from our barricade anything we could carry, up to the position held by H Troop." This did not weaken "M" Company's position, for as Taylor said, "our barricade was perhaps longer than was actually needed for the number of men behind it." Arriving at Benteen's position he described the situation there, saying that "Benteen's men were all lieing *[sic]* flat on the ground with no protection at all that I saw, and no evidence of any fortifying the night before by that troop."[33]

Returning to "M" Company's position, Taylor said that "a few moments later, F.C. Mann, a civilian packer, lieing *[sic]* not over two feet from me was shot in the head and instantly killed, he had been doing some long-range shooting, and raising his head just a little above the works for another shot, was struck, and expired without a sound."[34] Sgt. Roy also described this incident, but stated that Mann was killed on "A" Company's line, which suggests that "A" and "M" Companies were positioned next to each other.[35]

About 9:30 a.m., according to Lt. Edgerly, the Indians made "a desperate attempt to rout us. This was first directed against that portion of the line held by troops "H" and "M," one Indian coming so close to Col. Benteen's line that he touched a soldier with his coup stick. Col. Benteen immediately charged and drove the Indians away from his part of the line and then came over near where Reno was, and from the high point where he stood, could see the Indians crawling up on our left. He called out to Reno telling him what he had just accomplished and that if the Indians were not driven away from our flank they would gather us in. Reno asked him if he could see the Indians. (Reno couldn't see them as he was lying down in a rifle pit like the rest of us). He replied, 'Yes; they are right over there,' pointing. Reno then said, 'If you can see them, give the order to charge.' Benteen said, 'All right. Get ready, men! Now charge! Give 'em hell!' and with a shout we charged amidst a shower of bullets which came from five directions. The Indians fled incontinently and as soon as Reno saw this he said, 'Get back to your holes.' Shortly after this charge the firing suddenly and almost entirely ceased, and a great many Indians went to the village, leaving only a few pickets who stayed behind prominent points encircling our command."[36]

Pvt. Petring said that just as they were getting ready for Benteen's charge, Pvt. Andrew Moore was shot in the kidneys, and Pvt. Hugh McGonigle, also of Company "G," said that he had warned Moore to kneel when he was taking aim to fire, but that Moore said he could not take good aim that way. Accordingly, McGonigle said, Moore became careless and would rise up to fire and was soon shot in the body and killed.[37]

During this respite in the firing, Sgt. Roy said, "we dragged up more dead horses and extended our line up toward Benteen's position and gave better protection to the men."

THE BATTLE ON THE BLUFFS 93

As the sun rose higher, the heat intensified, and the men — especially the wounded — suffered from the lack of water, although, according to Sgt. Roy, "a little rain fell about noon, and the men held ponchos to catch some of it but did not get much."

"We became thirsty," Roy said, "and chewed grass to get saliva in our mouths, and [Pvt. Cornelius] Crowley went insane from thirst and did not recover for some time. We had to tie him fast."[38]

The need for water became critical, and nineteen troopers, responding to the cries of the wounded, volunteered to make the dangerous trek to the river. Some of the officers felt that a smaller force would have a better chance, and the number was reduced to twelve: Sgt. Roy, Pvts. Bancroft, Gilbert and Harris of Company "A," Pvts. Coleman and Boren of Company "B," Peter Thompson of Company "C," Theodore Goldin of Company "G," Saddler Otto Voit of Company "H," Michael Madden of Company "K," James Wilber and James Tanner of Company "M."[39]

Five sharpshooters were chosen to accompany the twelve and provide covering fire: Sgt. Henry Fehler of Company "A," Sgt. George Geiger, Blacksmith Henry Mecklin and Pvt. Charles Windolph, all of "H" Company, and Pvt. Edward Pigford of Company "M."

"In going down from the top of the bluff we had to run across an open space about 100 yards wide to get to the head of the ravine," Sgt. Roy recounted later. "From here to the river we were concealed from the Sioux. We got down to the mouth of the ravine and could see Indians in the brush on the opposite bank of the river, but we did not want to shoot, to bring on an engagement. Madden was the third man to rush for the water and was hit and [his] leg broke, but he crawled back to cover unassisted.

"I was fifth man to dash for the water," Roy continued. "The first man, whose name I do not remember, came back with a kettle full and we all took a drink, the first in 36 hours. I think Wilber was fourth, and he was wounded. After Madden was hit, he crawled back and we gave him water and nursed him and there was an intermission of about one-half hour before anyone went again. Altogether we were there in the ravine about an hour getting water. We would rush and fill the kettle from the river and then fill canteens from the kettles.

"In about one and one-half hours after starting we got back to the top of the hill with water, and [Lt.] Varnum was put guard over it. Dr. Porter issued water to the wounded, but there was still not enough to give them all they craved for."[40]

It is not clear whether Pvt. Tanner received his fatal wound as a water party volunteer or as one of those who participated in Benteen's charge. James Ryan, 1st Sergeant of Tanner's Company ("M"), said that Tanner was badly wounded in the charge, and that he, and three others, "rushed to his assistance, rolled him into [a] blanket, and made quick tracks in getting him from the side of the bluffs to where our wounded lay."

Ryan went on to say that "after placing Tanner with the rest of the wounded, he died in a few minutes," which would be on June 26. As Tanner's 1st Sergeant, Ryan's account should be the most authoritative, yet the roster of the regiment states that Tanner, wounded on the 26th, died the following day. Adding to the confusion is Walter Camp's inclusion of Tanner as a member of the water party which took place *after* Benteen's charge.[41]

A similar situation concerns Pvt. Wilber. Sgt. Roy said he was wounded with the water party, while Pvt. Rutten claimed Wilber was wounded in Benteen's charge. Walter Camp, who interviewed Wilber (whose real name was James W. Darcy), said that he was wounded in the left leg while attempting to get to the river with the water party.[42]

During the afternoon it was noted that the enemy fire was

decreasing, and about 3:00 or 4:00 o'clock it was reduced to a sniping action only. Following this, the Indians set the grass on the riverside of the bluffs afire, and when the smoke cleared the troops on the hill were astonished at the sight below them. The entire valley was choked with a procession of Indians and their pony herds heading south. The moving village remained in sight for hours, wending its way toward the Big Horn Mountains.

That night the last of the survivors hiding in the timber since Reno's retreat: Lt. DeRudio, Pvt. O'Neill, Interpreter Gerard and scout William Jackson, rejoined their comrades on the bluffs. For the forces of Reno and Benteen, the battle was over.

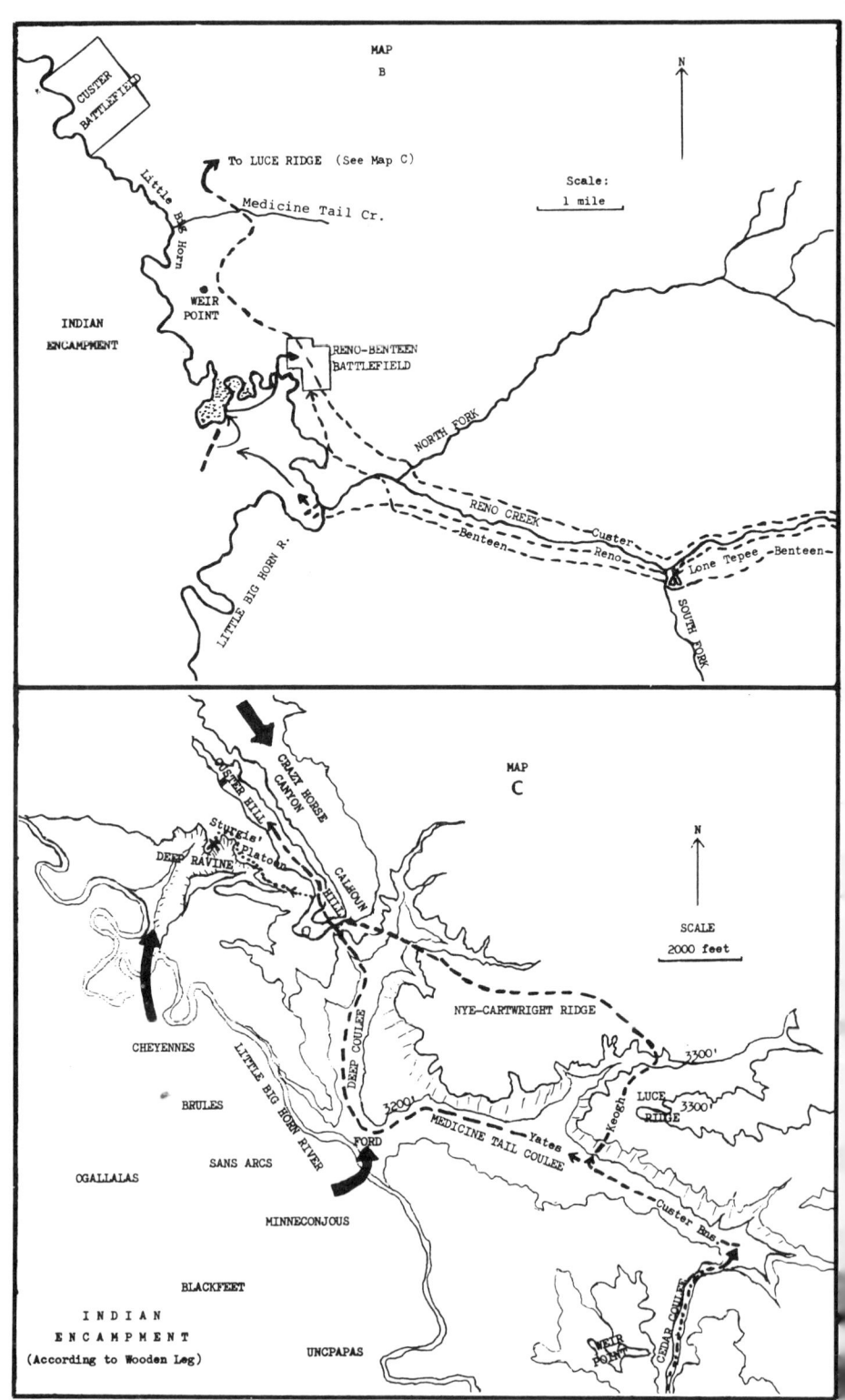

CHAPTER SEVEN
"The Mystery"

We approach the reconstruction of the final phase of the Custer Battle with some hesitancy, for "only fools rush in where angels fear to tread." Any attempt to unravel the tangled threads of Custer's action confronts us, at last, with "The Mystery." All the military witnesses to that action died there that day, and we are left with the fragmentary, and often contradictory testimony of the Indians who fought there. We know the "Who, What, Where and When," and the "Why" we will explore later. The mute bodies of the slain, and the scattered relics found on the battlefield, offer only meager clues to help us answer the "How," and it continues to elude us despite the many theories that have been presented to us over the past century as the "final solution" to the Mystery.

It is a well known fact that two or more persons, faced with the same evidence, can — and frequently do — arrive at different and even conflicting conclusions. The philosophers attribute this phenomenon to "the doctrine of the relativity of knowledge," a rather high-sounding phrase which means that human knowledge is relative to the limited nature of the human mind and the conditions which influence it — that the only things the mind can "know" are the *effects* which those things produce upon the mind, and not what the things themselves *are*.

Yet it is possible — perhaps even probable — that somewhere in the pile of theories of what really happened that day, the truth has already been exposed by one of us, and the rest of us have merely failed to discern it! But that, of course, is the essence of Mystery; not that truth is unknowable, but that it is hidden to minds that are closed to it.

Before we begin, we must accept certain basic premises:

1. Custer's march northward along the bluffs east of the Little Big Horn was for the purpose of *attacking* the hostiles. That should go without saying, but still must be said and accepted.

2. Custer made this movement still under the impression that the Indians were trying to escape. The information which Gerard passed on to Custer through Cooke that the Indians were "showing fight instead of running away" does not in any way affect this premise. Certainly Custer knew that the Indians would offer some resistance to Reno's charge in order to "buy time" for the non-combatants to escape. Such a rear-guard action was to be expected, and had the Indians not resisted Reno there would have been good reason to suspect (as Reno says he did, in fact) that the hostiles were simply luring him into a trap.[1]

3. Custer's strategy, then, was to support Reno's advance either by a flanking attack, or by getting ahead of the retreating Indians and cutting them off. Such a maneuver always has a demoralizing effect upon the enemy. B.H. Liddell Hart, in his excellent work, "Strategy," said that for the past two thousand years of known military history, successful campaigns have come as the result of the "dislocation of the enemy's balance, both psychological and physical, by means of a strategic indirect approach."[2] Custer made full use of this tried and true military principle at the Battle of the Washita in 1868, and at the time the decision was made he had no known reason to suspect that it would not be equally effective at the Little Big

Horn. Hindsight, of course, proves that the strategy failed here because Custer was operating on the basis of what is now known to have been erroneous information. Whether we believe that he *should* have known the true situation is a judgment that does not properly belong here and will be dealt with later.

If we can accept these premises as being true, so far as it is possible for us to recognize the truth, we then have a theoretical basis on which to build our reconstruction. From this point on we may very well be led in different directions, for the conflicting recollections of the hostiles and the fragmentary theories of the Reno-Benteen survivors are all open to individual interpretation. The apparent variance found in the Indian accounts can be partially explained by the fact that each warrior could describe only that part of the action in which he participated. His perspective, then, was unique and subjective. The action itself covered more than a square mile of topography, and no single warrior could have witnessed every phase of the action. Even the ubiquitous Wooden Leg, who apparently moved around the area to a greater extent than any other warrior whose account is known, could not describe everything that happened there that day, and the hostiles' ignorance of military strategy and tactics could easily confuse them and lead them to reach false conclusions. Yet the story cannot be told without reference to these sources for they are the only ones we have. Relying on one source exclusively can lead us astray, while ignoring a source simply because it fails to support our personal thesis can result in a distorted picture of the action. Perhaps we need to accept one more premise: that the analysis of *any* serious, informed student of the battle, trying to make the quantum leap from the known to the unknown without prejudgment, is just as valid as that of *any other* seeker, for in the face of Mystery we are all, at best, only theorists. With that in mind, we offer one more possible scenario:

As Trumpeter Martin rode off with his message to Benteen and Custer's battalion disappeared down the ravine, Bouyer and Curly remained on the high ridges of Weir Point, observing Reno's battalion in the valley below.[3] What information did Custer have regarding Reno's situation? We cannot say with certainty, of course, but we can evaluate the evidence available as to what he may have known. Unfortunately, the only available evidence is the testimony of the Crow scout, Curly, and in reviewing it we find it highly contradictory. Whether this reveals Curly as an unreliable witness, or whether the fault lies with his various interpreters, we cannot know. We can, however, test his stories by placing them within the context of our time-frame, thus separating the possible from the impossible.

As stated in Chapter Four we estimated that Reno began his charge at 3:10 p.m., halted to form the skirmish line at 3:20, and remained there 15 minutes before moving into the timber at approximately 3:35 p.m.

Custer had turned north at about 3:00 o'clock, arriving at the ridge northeast of Reno's Hill 15 minutes later, at 3:15, where he was seen by some of Reno's men who were charging down the valley. The Custer battalion then proceeded north at a trot for three-quarters of a mile, reaching the head of Cedar Coulee at about 3:20. There was a brief halt here while Custer called Martin and gave him the oral message for Benteen. Then Cooke stopped the messenger, telling him to wait while he wrote the message on a sheet of notebook paper, then sent him on his way as the battalion moved down Cedar Coulee and out of the sight of the troops in the valley. Meanwhile, Bouyer had dismissed three of the Crow scouts, and taking Curly with him, had set out toward Weir Point, a quarter of a mile ahead and to the left of Cedar Coulee, reaching the top about the same time that Martin left the command (3:25 p.m.), and the battalion started down the ravine.

From this high vantage point Bouyer had observed that Reno's command was engaged, which indicates that the soldiers were still in the open — on the skirmish line — for if they had moved into the timber Bouyer could not have seen them at all. The reader will recall that at some point in Bouyer's observation, which in Curly's words was "some little time," Bouyer became excited and waved his hat. The only explanation for this is that he saw the troops move from the skirmish line into the timber, a defensive move made necessary by the increasing number of Indians around the soldiers. In the timber they had an excellent defensive position which still threatened the enemy and would occupy their full attention for quite some time. Bouyer's reaction to this movement would then make sense out of Curly's description of it: that "at the sight of this, Bouyer could hardly restrain himself and shouted and waved his hat excitedly for some little time."

If this had been Curly's only account we would have to deduce from it that when Bouyer later joined Custer in Medicine Tail Coulee, he told the General that Reno was still engaging the enemy and that the situation was well under control. However, in an interview on July 19, 1910, interpreted by Fred Old Horn, Curly said he saw Reno's retreat, and that Bouyer, after joining Custer, "probably told him that Reno had been defeated, for Bouyer did a whole lot of talking to Custer when he joined him and kept talking while they were riding side by side."[4]

Three years later, on September 30, 1913, Thomas Le Forge interpreted for Curly in another Camp interview with the scout. Here again Curly said, "I had then seen Reno defeated in the bottom and discussed it with Mitch. I saw Mitch say something to General Custer when we met him and presumed that he must have informed him about Reno's situation."[5]

Could Curly have seen Reno's retreat? Not according to our timetable, for that action took place from 3:55 to 4:10 p.m. By that time Custer had left Medicine Tail Coulee, as will be developed later, and Curly would have left Weir Point — the last place from which Reno's valley fight could be seen — at least ten minutes before the retreat began.

Commenting on Curly's 1908 interview, Mr. Camp wrote that Bouyer and Curly then moved north toward Medicine Tail Coulee, coming down from Weir Point, and that "Bouyer began looking over east to see what Custer was doing. Presently Custer and command showed up, in the distance, coming down the coulee, and Bouyer said they had better go down to the command and see what the orders were." Camp is here summarizing what Curly said in that interview, and continued: "Curly gave me this information on the ground. We were then beyond the high point and by looking east, or possibly a little north of east, could see up Medicine Tail Coulee quite a distance. I do not find in my notes the positive statement of Curly that Custer had halted in the coulee, and it did not then occur to me to ask, but the fact that Bouyer and Curly started over east to join Custer (these two being between Custer and the river) must indicate that Custer had halted the command, otherwise Mitch and Curly would have waited for him to come along, and joined him in the coulee opposite where they were or at a point nearer the river. They were not directly in front of Custer — that is, not in the coulee — but were much nearer the river than Custer." Camp also reported that Curly said Custer was a mile from the river and that he and Bouyer were about a half-mile below him.[6]

As stated in the premises at the beginning of this chapter, Custer rode north with the intention of attacking the Indians, still believed to be fleeing. Yet now we find Custer's battalion halted in Medicine Tail Coulee (actually closer to two miles from the river rather than Curly's estimate of one mile). Why the halt? One obvious reason would surely be to give the horses

THE MYSTERY

a "breather," and allow the men time to tighten the cinches and prepare for action. They had just completed a long and tiring march, and the fact that somewhere along the way four troopers had been forced to drop out of the column when their horses became exhausted, indicates that a "break" period was needed. But there is one further reason for the halt: to divide the command into two battalions now that action was finally imminent. We do not *know* that this was done, but the subsequent action — and some of the Indian testimony — makes such a division the only obvious explanation. Many students of the battle believe that Col. Keogh, the ranking captain with Custer, was given command of his own company, "I" and also Companies "L" (Calhoun's) and "C" (Tom Custer's). The second battalion then would be Company "E" (Smith's) and "F," both under the latter company's captain, Col. Yates. There is some disagreement about whether "C" Company was with Keogh or Yates and there is some evidence that would support either opinion. Our own hypothesis is that Company "C" was itself divided into its two platoons, one assigned to Keogh and the other to Yates. This would not only equalize the strength of the two battalions, but also would explain the fact that a substantial number of "C" Company bodies were found on the two ends of the battleridge: some with "L" and "I" Companies, and others found with the Custer group which included "E" and "F."

It is necessary here to return to our timetable. Custer had started down Cedar Coulee at about 3:25 p.m. The ravine is 1600 yards long (nearly a mile) from its head to its mouth. The gait of the battalion is not known, but it was probably a walk, and when possible, a trot, which would bring the command to the flat area in Medicine Tail where the two coulees join at approximately 3:35 p.m. The halt here, variously estimated from 15 to 45 minutes, was probably no longer than 20 minutes.

Bouyer and Curly joined the command during this halt and Bouyer reported to Custer on what he had seen from Weir Point.

At the head of his two battalions, Custer set out down the coulee at about 3:55 p.m., the time when Reno began his retreat, and reached a point about one mile from the river where he again called a halt, presumably to confer with his battalion commanders. Then, ordering Yates' battalion forward, he led Keogh's command to the right, ascending the north slope of the coulee to the ridge which forms the northern rim of Medicine Tail. It is probable that Curly was dismissed on this ridge for the Crows were told to leave when action became imminent. Why Curly had not been sent away earlier, with the other Crow scouts, is not known. Perhaps Bouyer, the leader of the Crow contingent, had been given authority to dismiss them at his own discretion. It is appropriate to have Curly leave the column at this time, for his testimony regarding the events that followed is impossible to accept at face value.

The ridge along the north rim of Medicine Tail is called "Luce Ridge," in honor of Supt. Edward Luce who, in the 1940s, discovered a number of cartridge cases there, and the spacing of them, in his professional opinion as a former cavalryman, indicated a dismounted skirmish. In 1951, Major Luce escorted this writer to that ridge and pointed out where the shell casings had been found, and where a cavalry spur and part of a McClellan saddle (as well as other artifacts) had been found subsequent to his original discovery. The ridge presents an excellent overview of the ford across the Little Big Horn at the mouth of Medicine Tail Coulee, and of the north end of the valley. Needless to say, the troops on these eastern ridges would now be visible to the Indians also, especially to the women and children who had run across the river at the ford when it was thought that Reno would charge through the village. When he stopped, most of these non-combatants returned to their lodges, but there must have been enough of them in the vicinity to see the soldiers coming now from the east.

The move down Medicine Tail from the point where Custer first entered it, and the ascent to Luce Ridge probably totals a little over one mile, and should have been accomplished in about 15 minutes. If we add 5 minutes for the brief halt just before the two battalions moved out independently of each other we can place the arrival of the Keogh battalion on Luce Ridge at about 4:15 p.m., only moments after Reno's beleaguered troops had arrived on the bluffs, now being surrounded by hostiles to the west and north of his position.

How, then, do we account for the firing by the troops on Luce Ridge over two miles away? The answer, we believe can be found in the testimony of our old friend, Wooden Leg, whom we left upstream as one of those pursuing Reno's retreating forces.

When the last of Reno's men reached the bluffs Wooden Leg returned to the west side of the river and joined those who were searching the bodies of the slain. He had already captured a rifle, and was pleased to find two boxes of ammunition for it in the saddlebags of a dead horse. He tells us that "the soldiers had gone up gulches and a backbone ridge to the top of a steep and high hill," and that Indians were all about them. "Shots were going toward them and coming from them." He then decided to join those on the bluffs, "going around to the left or north side of the place where were the soldiers. From our hilltop position I fired a few shots from my newly-obtained rifle.

"I had been there only a short time when somebody said to me: 'Look! Yonder are other soldiers.' I saw them on distant hills down the river and on our same side of it. The news then spread quickly among us. Indians began to ride in that direction. Some went along the hills, others went down to cross the river and follow the valley. I took this course."

Riding through the encampment to the Cheyenne circle he

"could see lots of Indians out on the hills across to the east side of the river and fighting the other soldiers there." Undoubtedly these were the same Indians whom Wooden Leg had left on the bluffs north of Reno and who had taken a short-cut along the bluffs following Custer's trail to Medicine Tail Coulee. As they entered the coulee, they must have begun firing at the troops who were now atop Luce Ridge. We have estimated that this battalion reached the ridge by 4:15 p.m., shortly after Reno's men reached their hill position. The Indians on the bluffs north of Reno Hill could not have seen Custer's troop until Keogh's battalion left the shelter of Medicine Tail Coulee and ascended Luce Ridge, which means that these troops were seen at 4:15 or a few minutes later. Riding furiously north to meet this new threat should have been accomplished by the warriors in not more than fifteen minutes, certainly not much more than 4:30 p.m.

Wooden Leg probably reached his tribal circle in about ten minutes. There, at his family lodge, he renewed his "medicine" while his father caught a fresh horse for him. When he was ready he "looked a few moments at the battling Indians and soldiers across the river on the hills to the northeastward. More and more Indians were flocking from the camps to that direction. Some were yet coming along the hills from where the first soldiers (Reno's) had stopped. The soldiers now in view were spreading themselves into lines along a ridge. The Indians were on lower ridges in front of them, between them and the river, and were moving on around up a long coulee to get behind the white men."

The troopers who were "spreading themselves into lines along a ridge" were obviously the dismounted skirmishers who had left their expended cartridge cases there for Major Luce to find nearly seventy years later.

As the Indians moved up Medicine Tail Coulee, most of them "dismounted and crept along the gullies afoot," according to Wooden Leg. "The soldiers had come along a high ridge about two miles east from the Cheyenne camp," he continued. "While they were yet on the far-out ridge a few Sioux and Cheyennes had exchanged shots with them at long distance, without anybody being hurt."[7]

The skirmish line may have been established to cover the movement of the battalion to an adjacent ridge, slightly higher, which begins 1000 yards almost due north of the westernmost extension of Luce Ridge and continues for about 1300 yards northwest in a direct line toward the southeast corner of the Custer Battlefield fence. The army shell casings found along it in profuse numbers were first discovered by Mr. Joe Blummer in the 1920s. In the late 1930s Lt. Col. Edward L. Nye and Mr. R.G. Cartwright found even more artifacts, and in 1943, Cartwright and Major Luce found several more.

Separating the two ridges is an extensive coulee that rises about one mile due north (and a little east) of the mouth of Cedar Coulee where Custer entered Medicine Tail. This ravine is a tributary of Medicine Tail, and as it curves southwest to join the larger coulee it forms the western extension of Luce Ridge. As part of the battalion moved across the upper reaches of this tributary to reach Nye-Cartwright Ridge, the coulee probably started to fill with Indians trying to encircle the troops. This might be what Wooden Leg was talking about when he said that the Indians "were moving around up a long coulee to get behind the white men."

Those soldiers who had already crossed over to Nye-Cartwright probably took a position enabling them to see into the coulee and fired volleys into and down the ravine, clearing it for the safe passage of the rest of the troops.[8]

The volley firing heard by the Reno-Benteen forces took place after Lt. Hare set out to bring in the packtrain. As stated previously in Chapter Six, Hare left about 4:30 p.m., ten minutes after Benteen joined Reno, and returned at 4:50 p.m.

We then have a twenty minute time-frame in which we can place the volley firing from Nye-Cartwright Ridge which caused so much consternation on Reno Hill. It took place shortly after Hare left, for when he returned at 4:50, he saw "D" Company already three-quarters of a mile north on their way to Weir Point. Weir, followed by his company, would have had to leave Reno Hill about ten minutes before 4:50 and they did not leave immediately upon hearing the firing which must have started by 4:35. Godfrey said it continued for a long time — scattered fire, presumably — for he went on to say "We heard two distinct volleys, which excited some surprise, and if I mistake not, brought about the remark from some one that 'Custer was giving it to them for all he is worth.'" It was after this, according to Godfrey, that Weir and Edgerly decided to move toward the sound of the guns, as all proper military custom demanded. The volleys were fired, then, at approximately 4:40 p.m. and we can reasonably place Custer, apparently with the Keogh battalion, on the ridge we know as Nye-Cartwright at that time.

One of the reasons we have abandoned the Crow scout Curly as a witness is that none of his testimony touches upon the encounters that took place on the ridges to the east of the village. In all his accounts, Curly insisted that Custer rode straight for the ford at the mouth of Medicine Tail Coulee, that he tried to cross the stream (in one story he said Custer did cross), and that he was forced to retreat to the ridge where he died.[9] Dr. Kuhlman, one of those who disputed this, attributed Curly's account to Mr. Camp's presupposition that Custer did attack at the ford — that his leading questions confused Curly and he said what he believed Camp *wanted* him to say. The same criticism may be leveled at a number of others who interviewed certain of the Sioux and Cheyennes who were present at the battle. There is much validity to this criticism by Kuhlman, shared by this writer, and it can be made without in any way challenging the integrity of Mr. Camp himself or belittling his many outstanding contributions to the study of the Battle of the Little Big Horn. Camp had no problem in his interviews with the surviving soldiers, which suggests that part of his trouble in the Indian interviews was probably the ineptitude of the interpreters.

Yet the belief that Custer had attacked at the ford was widely held following the battle and is still held by many students today. When we consider the bold nature of Custer in warfare, and remember that he had ridden north for the sole purpose of attacking, it would certainly seem to be the most obvious maneuver. One of the first to assume that Custer had tried to cross the river at the mouth of the coulee was Colonel Benteen. In a letter to his wife, written July 4, he said he was "of the opinion that nearly — if not all of the five companies got into the village — but were driven out immediately." Yet at the conclusion of the letter we read that he had already changed his mind: "The latest and probably the correct account of the battle is that none of Custer's commands got into the village at all."[10] At the 1879 Court of Inquiry Benteen's conclusions had lost their ambivalence when he said that if Custer "had gone down to the river and was attacked there, there would have been horses and men killed there, but there were none." In response to a question by the Recorder, Lt. Jesse Lee, as to how close Custer came to the river, Benteen answered, "Three furlongs I should say." As a furlong is 220 yards, the distance then was 660 yards or over one-third of a mile.

There is, however, testimony from some of the hostiles supporting the theory that Custer attacked at the ford. The Cheyenne warrior, Tall Bull, although admitting that he did not see the first part of the Custer fight, said that Custer got onto the flat *near the ford* (italics mine, CdB) within easy gunshot of the village and was driven back by the Indians. "By the time I got there," he told Walter Camp, "they had driven the soldiers to the first rise" (here Camp inserted: "where Foley lay") and they were going up the ridge to the right of Custer coulee and the Indians driving them." He then makes the statement that "the soldiers did not make any charge on the Indians during the Custer fight."[11]

He Dog, an Ogallala, returned to the village from the Reno fight by passing through the Uncpapa camp to his own tribal circle southwest of the Cheyenne camp.

"Then we looked and saw other soldiers coming on the big hill right over east," he said. "They kept right on down the river and crossed Medicine Tail coulee and onto a little rise." (Camp inserted: 'the first rise above the flat south of the mouth of Medicine Tail where Foley was found.') "Here Custer's line was scattered all along parallel with the river from Foley to Butler. When Custer passed near Ford B, he was moving as though to reach the lower end of our camp."[12]

"Ford B," of course, was the designation for the ford at the mouth of Medicine Tail Coulee. The reference to Foley was to the only body found in the vicinity of the ford. Sergeant Roy said, "When we went to bury the dead on June 28 we did not follow Dry Creek (Medicine Tail Coulee) to the river, but cut straight across to the battlefield going over the little rise between the two coulees" (the north and south branches of Medicine Tail). "The first dead body we came to was that of Corpl. John Foley. I heard several say: 'There lies Foley of C Company.' I saw him and recognized him easily, as he had bald head and black hair. He was of middle age and I knew him well. Foley was at least three-fourths mile in advance of the first group of dead at C. (The reference to "C" is to a map designation which Camp obviously used in his interviews for the southwestern extension of Calhoun Ridge).

"The next body we came to was that of Sergt. Butler, and from him to first group of dead at C the distance was considerable. He lay probably one-half way from Foley to C. There was no dead horse near either Foley or Butler."[13]

The Sioux warrior Standing Bear, in another Camp interview, said that Custer approached the village over "low ground to the east, down a kind of dry coulee. As soon as the soldiers came in sight they halted and apparently were preparing for a charge." This must refer to the halt made by Custer before he turned north. Standing Bear continued: "Finally the soldiers advanced very near to the river, but before they could cross were engaged by the Indians and forced back to the ridge where the main fight took place." These are Camp's words, of course, summarizing his interview with Standing Bear, and they continue as follows: [He] "says as soon as Custer came in sight and halted, some of the Indians crossed over, but he advanced against this resistance nearly to the river before it became strong enough to check him."

Camp also reports Standing Bear as saying that Custer's soldiers did not fire into the village, and that they did not fight by companies, but were "altogether all the time."[14]

As pointed out previously, it is difficult to tell which are Standing Bear's words and which are Camp's, for Mr. Camp was convinced that Custer had gone to the river. Standing Bear's statement that the troops did not fight by companies might well be explained by the fact that he saw the Yates' battalion head straight for the ford and that this imminent threat occupied his full attention, thereby failing to see the other battalion turn north and away from the river. It should also be pointed out that in the Indian testimony, when they speak of "Custer," they do not refer to the General himself, but simply to his troops. It has been adequately reiterated by other writers that the Indians did not even know that Custer was there, supposing the soldiers to be the same ones they had fought on the Rosebud, June 17.

This testimony of Tall Bull, He Dog and Standing Bear tends to support the theory that Custer attempted to attack the camps at the Medicine Tail Coulee ford. However, there is also testimony from other hostiles that contradicts this. Gall, an Uncpapa warrior chief, said that Custer's battalion never reached the river — that Custer was attacked fully three-quarters of a mile back from the river, near the crest of the ridge lining the coulee he was descending, and was forced back, step by step, at right angles to his former course to the summit of the battleridge where the present monument stands.[15] We have already heard the testimony of Wooden Leg which seems to support that of Gall. There is other testimony on both sides of this issue, but these few should suffice to illustrate that there are obviously two different schools of thought, and both seem convinced of the validity of their claims. As for the opinions of the military, we have already heard from Benteen, whose conclusion was echoed by Godfrey: "No bodies of men or horses were found anywhere near the ford, and these facts are conclusive to my mind that Custer did not go to the ford with any body of men."[16]

There is also some silent testimony to consider, and that is the physical evidence found at the mouth of Medicine Tail Coulee. The recent archeological work done there (and earlier) has unearthed three 45.70 caliber army cartridge cases on the west bank of the river, and two more on the east bank. About 250 yards east of the ford, sixteen additional cartridges have been found.[17] This total of twenty-one expended rifle shells at or near the ford is hardly indicative of any kind of military action, and can be more reasonably attributed to the fact that some of the Indians (Wooden Leg being one of them) had captured carbines from Reno's battlefield in the valley fight and had used them in their long-distance firing from the ford at the troops to the east. At any rate, the discovery of small numbers of scattered cartridge cases is hardly solid evidence on which to build a theory of military action.[18]

The ford at the mouth of Medicine Tail Coulee provided the easiest access to both the village and the coulee. Following the battle most of the Indians, warriors and non-combatants alike, used the ford to return to their tribal circles. The spoils of the battle included not only the weapons and clothing of the soldiers, but also their horses, which would certainly account for the tracks of shod horses found at the ford.

Stories of bodies found at or near the ford cannot be substantiated, and it appears that the closest body was that of Corporal Foley. A number of independent Indian accounts tell of the soldier who, at the battle's end, attempted to escape by riding south from the battleridge. Pursued by a small group of warriors, the soldier realized that escape was impossible and shot himself in the head. The body, later identified as that of Foley, was found 800 feet east of the river.[19]

At least four severed heads were found in the village after the battle, but there is disagreement as to whether any decapitated bodies were found there.[20] Some of the heads may have been taken from Reno's men in the valley, but there is direct testimony that at least one came from Custer's men. Wooden Leg mentioned one soldier wearing buckskins whose "head was cut off and gone."[21] Lt. James Porter of Co. "I," whose body was never identified, is known to have been wearing buckskins and was probably the man seen by Wooden Leg. Needless to say, this kind of mutilation would certainly have made identification impossible.

In view of the evidence cited — oral and physical — it would appear that no troops reached the river and that no engagement took place at the ford. Yet the testimony does indicate that a movement of troops was made *toward* the river, and this could only have been done by the Yates battalion.

When the Keogh battalion turned to the north out of Medicine Tail Coulee on its way to Luce Ridge, Yates and his battalion may have continued down the coulee toward the river, although it is possible that the entire command ascended the ridge and that Yates was sent toward the river from there. This latter possibility becomes more probable when we consider the testimony of the Cheyenne, White Shield. While he was still in the village, dressing for battle, he "saw Custer's troops in seven groups approaching the river," and said they were "still at a distance." Later in the action, Grinnell, apparently still quoting White Shield," said that "three of the troops had lost their horses, but four still had theirs."[22] If this is true, then another company had been divided into its two platoons for the entire command numbered only five companies. As will be developed later, it is probable that Co. "E" was the other group operating on the platoon system. Lining up his five troops in seven groups atop Nye-Cartwright Ridge, Custer presented a far more intimidating threat to the village below, and apparently it worked, at least for a time, for the Cheyenne Mad Wolf said to White Shield, "No one must charge on the soldiers now; they are too many."[23]

The movement of the Yates battalion toward the river crossing was a logical tactical move, designed to distract the enemy and focus their attention on the more immediate threat while the other battalion on the ridge maneuvered northwestward, presumably to outflank the Indians and attack from the north. It is doubtful that any attack was made upon the troops near the river until after they had turned away and rode up the north branch of Medicine Tail, called "Deep Coulee," for He Dog said, "There was no fighting; fifteen or twenty Sioux on east side of river, and some of [the] soldiers replied, but not much shooting there."[24] Indians never confused courage with folly, and would not attack an organized force head-on. They would, however (as Reno learned), attack at the first sign of weakness or indecision, or when the troops turned away from them. Yates had apparently accomplished his purpose, which was to threaten the village and keep more of the hostiles from crossing the river. Moving up Deep Coulee, he then swung to the left and headed for what is now known as Calhoun Ridge, the eastern extension of the Custer Battleridge. Here he halted his command, and Custer, with Keogh's battalion, moved along Nye-Cartwright ridge to the upper reaches of Deep Coulee to control this access, now rapidly filling up with Indians. Custer apparently ordered additional volleys fired into the coulee, for Gerard, who was hiding in the timber in the valley, heard this firing, as did Herendeen.[25] The two battalions now held both the high points bordering the upper reaches of Deep Coulee and it is possible that Wooden Leg's description of the action involved this portion of the battlefield:

"Most of the Indians were working around the ridge now occupied by the soldiers. We were lying down in gullies and behind sagebrush hillocks. The shooting at first was at a distance, but we kept creeping in closer all around the ridge. Bows and arrows were in use more than guns. The slow long-distance fighting was kept up for about an hour and a half, I believe."[26]

Why did Custer remain on Nye-Cartwright Ridge so long? He had ascended this ridge because it afforded him his first glimpse of this end of the valley, and from it he saw that the Indians were not running away. His brother Boston, who probably joined the battalion in Cedar Coulee, had surely told the General of Benteen's location at the time he passed him at 1:15. Knowing that Benteen was on his trail in compliance with the order to "Come on — be quick — bring packs," an order that Benteen should have received an hour ago, Custer realized that he must remain at an elevation which would enable Benteen to see him. Having arrived on Luce Ridge at 4:15, then moving to Nye-Cartwright about 4:40 p.m., acording to our timetable, he continued to wait for Benteen to arrive. Wooden Leg's statement that the long-distance fighting continued for about an hour and a half probably means that it started after Keogh reached Luce Ridge at about 4:15, and continued until about 5:45 p.m. Finally Custer must have concluded that Benteen was not going to come, and the two battalions were rejoined as Keogh and Custer moved across the coulee to Calhoun Ridge.

Wooden Leg continues: "After the long time of the slow fighting, about forty of the soldiers came galloping from the east part of the ridge down toward the river, toward where most of the Cheyennes and many Ogallalas were hidden. The Indians ran back to a deep gulch."[27]

This incident, vividly described by Wooden Leg and supported in detail by Kate Bighead, has perplexed many students of the battle, some rejecting it out of hand. Can it be explained? We think it can; when Custer's two battalions were joined on Calhoun Ridge it was obviously decided that Yates' battalion would march along the ridge and take control of the northwest end of it while Keogh's battalion would occupy the southeast end, Calhoun Ridge. Most of the hostile firing was coming from the slope of the battleridge on the side facing the river, and as Yates moved along the top of the ridge, a platoon of "E" Company, under Lt. Sturgis, moved from the east along the slope below the crest of the ridge, following the north side of a ravine that further down opens into a steep-sided gully. His purpose was to flush out any Indians hiding on the slope in its many depressions under cover of the sagebrush so that Yates' battalion could move along the ridge without this kind of harassment of the hostiles. What none of the soldiers knew was that this deep ravine was filled with Cheyennes and Ogallalas, and as the platoon approached their hiding place they ran down into the deepest part of the ravine where they could not be visible from above. Wooden Leg tells us, "the soldiers stopped and got off their horses when they arrived at a low ridge where the Indians had been. Lame White Man, the Southern Cheyenne chief, came on his horse and called to us to come back and fight. In a few minutes the warriors were all around these soldiers."[28]

Lieutenant Sturgis, having seen no Indians, apparently assumed that the ravine was clear of them, otherwise the men would not have dismounted and stood there with their rifles still in the scabbards on their horses. By this time the rest of the battalion had reached Custer Hill and was being deployed as skirmishers at least a quarter of a mile north of Sturgis' platoon.

Kate Bighead, who had been watching this action from a ridge south of the deep ravine, said, "Lame White Man, the bravest Cheyenne warrior chief, stayed in hiding close to where the small band of soldiers got off their horses. From there he called to the young men, and they began creeping and dodging back to him. The Ogallala Sioux chiefs also called to their young men, and these also returned to the fight. Within a few minutes there were many hundreds of warriors wriggling along the gullies all around these soldiers."[29]

"Then Lame White Man called out: 'Come. We can kill them all,'" Wooden Leg said, and the Indians swarmed out of the gully around the protecting cover of a small hillock and by sheer weight of their numbers overwhelmed the platoon, forcing the men into the gully, then, standing on the edge of the ravine, they fired into the tangled mass of soldiers until nearly all were dead. A few men who survived the initial onslaught tried to escape by running up the gully toward Calhoun Hill, but one by one they were shot down.

Thirty-six men and two officers of "E" Company died with Custer, and if the troop was divided into equal platoons, Lt. Sturgis had 18 men with him. After the battle, 28 bodies were found in this ravine and some of those on top of the pile were identified as "F" Company troopers, men who at the last ran down the hill and were killed in or near the ravine.

The destruction of Sturgis' platoon of the Grey Horse Company probably took no more than fifteen minutes. If the movement of this platoon began shortly after it reached Calhoun Hill, it must have started about 6:00 p.m. Riding at a gallop to the point near the gully where it stopped, the platoon should have covered that half-mile in less than five minutes. A few minutes later, the attack began, and probably ended ten minutes later, at about 6:15 p.m., just as the Reno-Benteen command left Reno Hill for Weir Point.

The Uncpapa warrior chief, Crow King, may have been present with the Cheyennes and Ogallalas in this action. In 1886, David F. Barry was told by Gall, the Uncpapa warrior, "Crow King and Crazy Horse were afraid the soldiers that we had seen march in the direction of the north end of the camp, might kill our women and children. They went back the way they had come; their ponies were racing. Crow King turned to the right before he got to the north end and got in a deep gully and those soldiers (Custer's), could not see that this gully is so deep that no one can see you from there. This gully, the upper part, brought Crow King very close to the soldiers. Crazy Horse went to the extreme north end of the camp and then turned to his right and went up another very deep ravine and by following it, which he did, he came very close to the soldiers on their north side. Crow King was on their south side."[30]

Those familiar with the topography of the area will have no difficulty in following this account, for the "deep gully" can only be Deep Ravine, and the "deep ravine" chosen by Crazy Horse on the north side of the Battleridge can only be what is known as "Crazy Horse Canyon" today.

We also learn from this account that the attack on Keogh's battalion by Crazy Horse must have followed the annihilation of Sturgis' platoon within a very short time. The avenue of attack taken by this noted Ogallala warrior chief was the long and deep ravine that borders the northeast side of the Custer Battleridge, and leads directly to the Keogh-Calhoun positions. At about the same time, Gall and his Uncpapas attacked from the south. Calhoun's Company "L" had established a dismounted skirmish line with one platoon as the markers there clearly indicate, and were able to put up a successful defense against Gall for a short time. Meanwhile, Crazy Horse had struck Keogh's Company "I" and virtually destroyed it in a body, then sweeping over the ridge, struck Calhoun from the rear. A handful of the men from "I" and "L" were apparently able to make their way on foot to Custer's position at the other end of the ridge, for a few "L" Company troopers were found there. However, it is quite possible they were with Custer all along, for a number of men from other companies were on special assignment with headquarters and with all the other companies. Calhoun, and his lieutenant, John Crittenden, were found on the knoll of what is now Calhoun Hill. Keogh, found nearly a third of the way toward Custer Hill, lay close to his 1st Sergeant, Frank Varden, his trumpeter, John Patton, and Sgt. James Bustard; his leg had been broken, apparently by the same bullet that had wounded his horse, "Comanche," the only living creature found on the battlefield.[31] When he fell, his sergeants formed around him in a futile attempt to protect him.

Edwin Bobo, 1st Sergeant of Company "C," was also found near Keogh, and on the western extension of Calhoun Ridge, the bodies of other "C" Company non-commissioned officers were found: Sergeants August Finckle and Jeremiah Finley. The body of their officer, Lt. Henry Harrington, was never found or identified and may have been one of those decapitated.

All this must have occurred shortly after the destruction of Lt. Sturgis' platoon of "E" Company in the deep ravine south of Custer Hill, for Wooden Leg said that "the Indians took the guns of these soldiers and used them for shooting at the soldiers on the high ridge. I went back and got my horse and rode around beyond the east end of the ridge (Calhoun Hill). By the time I got there, all the soldiers there were dead."[32]

Kate Bighead made the same observation: "I started to go around the east end of the soldier ridge. Just then I saw lots of Indians running toward that end of the ridge, and the soldier horses there were running away. Pretty soon I saw that all of the white men were dead and the warriors were among them getting their guns." She went on to say that "The Indians crowded on westward along the ridge and along its two sides."[33]

The action now shifted to the last remaining troops of Custer's command: Company "F" and the two platoons of "C" and "E" Companies. Wooden Leg tells us: "I raced my horse to hurry around to the hillside north of the soldier ridge. The Indians there were all around a band of soldiers on the north slope. I got off my horse and fired two shots, at long distance, with my soldier gun. I did not shoot any more, because the sagebrush was full of Indians jumping up and down and crawling close to the soldiers, and I was afraid I might hit one of our own men."[34]

It was the beginning of the end. He Dog said that the "fight with Custer did not last much more than an hour, as nearly as I can estimate it,"[35] and he was probably right, for even during the action on the east end of the ridge, the Indians watching Custer were taking their toll of his men. The principal weapon in this long siege had been the bow and arrow, for as Wooden Leg explained it, "the arrows could be shot in a high and long curve, to fall upon the soldiers or their horses. An Indian using a gun had to jump up and expose himself long enough to shoot. The arrows falling upon the horses stuck in their backs and caused them to go plunging here and there, knocking down the soldiers."[36]

THE MYSTERY

Once the troops on Calhoun Ridge had been killed, all the Indians converged on the men on Custer Hill and casualties mounted quickly. On top of the knoll, now the leveled area where the Battle Monument stands, five or six "C" Company sorrels were shot to form a barricade.[37] It may have been about this time that Corporal Foley made his escape attempt by riding south past the ford where he shot himself. Another trooper, probably of Company "I," had apparently been bypassed by the Indians moving from the Keogh-Calhoun positions on their way to Custer Hill. Believing himself to be undetected, he started running for the ridge bordering the north side of Crazy Horse Canyon, a ridge that was filled with non-combatant spectators from the village. When the soldier realized the hopelessness of his attempt, he, too, shot himself. His marker may be seen today, all alone and some distance from the Custer Battleridge.

Tall Bull, the Cheyenne, told of a final desperate effort by some of the last men still alive on Custer Hill to escape by running down the slope. "They ran right through us into the deep gully," he said, "and this was the last of the fight, and the men were killed in the gully."[38] It was probably these last men, perhaps of "F" Company, who fell on top of the bodies of Sturgis' platoon. No effort was made by the burial party to remove these badly decomposed bodies on June 28, and their interment was accomplished by caving in the sides of the gully upon them. Captain McDougall, former commander of Company "E," was placed in charge of identifying and burying these men. Sgt. Roy said that he "helped to bury the bodies on [the] west slope of the ridge, and we wound up with E Troop men over near the gully. I then took sick to my stomach from the stench and went to the river to get a drink."[39]

Trumpeter Henry Dose of "G" Company had been assigned as an orderly to General Custer that day and may have been sent as a messenger at some time during the engagement, perhaps to repeat Custer's original message to Benteen to "Come on — be quick." His body was found half-way between Custer and Reno, according to Private Henry Petring, with arrows shot into his back and sides.[40]

When the last man was dead, the women and children rushed to the field to plunder and mutilate the dead bodies scattered all along the battleridge and below it. Nearly all of the soldiers were stripped, and clothing belonging to Lieutenants Sturgis and Porter, whose bodies were never found or at least never identified, was found on the site of the village. General Custer lay across the bodies of two troopers, unmutilated, shot in the left breast, and like many of the others, dispatched with a final shot to the head. Near him lay the bodies of Lt. Reily, Capt. Smith, and Lt. Col. Cooke. Custer's brother Tom, horribly mutilated, lay about twenty feet away, and his youngest brother, Boston, was found some distance down the slope with their nephew, Harry Armstrong Reed.

Private Dennis Lynch of "F" Company said that Chief Trumpeter Henry Voss and Sgt. John Vickory, assigned as Color Sergeant, were found near Custer, which sounds most likely, but Pvt. George Glenn said that Voss was found near the body of Mark Kellogg, the Bismarck *Tribune* correspondent, three-quarters of a mile down toward the river, "a stone's throw from the river." Lt. Mathey said that he buried Kellogg's body on June 29th, the day after the other burials took place; the body had been overlooked the previous day by those searching for the slain, and Mathey said it lay near a ravine between Custer and the river.[41]

Altogether, four officers were never identified: Lieutenants Porter of "I" Company, Sturgis of "E" Company, Harrington of "C" Company, and Dr. George Lord, Assistant Surgeon, whose medical kit was found in the village. However, Col. Richard E. Thompson, with Gibbon's command, stated quite positively that he had identified Lord's body, found 20 feet southeast of Custer's body on the hill.[42] Very few bodies of enlisted men were identified, and apparently very little effort was made to do so. The few identifications made were by other enlisted personnel who were looking for the bodies of friends, although Captain McDougall did identify the body of his former 1st Sergeant Edward Hohmeyer of "E" Company as one of those found in the ravine below the battleridge. Pvt. Tom "Boss" Tweed of "L" Company was identified by Pvt. Glenn, Pvt. Francis Hughes of "L" Company was found near Custer by Pvt. John Foley, and Sgt. Robert Hughes of "K" Company was identified by Captain McDougall near Sgt. Hohmeyer in the ravine.[43]

It was about 7:00 p.m. when the last shots were fired on Custer Hill, and the Indians, looking southeast, saw the troops under Reno and Benteen on Weir Point, three miles away, outlined against the horizon. As the troops turned away, heading back to Reno Hill, the victorious Indians rode toward them, their work on the Custer Battlefield now finished.

Was there a survivor of the Custer Battle? In Russell White Bear's last interview with Curly, the Crow scout said that Custer, "on reaching Medicine Tail Creek, halted his command, and here the men rearranged their saddles. Custer at this point gave a trooper a paper and after a brief conversation, the trooper rode away, heading north. This trooper rode a sorrel-roan horse."[44] The story could very well be true; Custer knew that Terry and Gibbon were now north of his position and he may have wanted Terry to know what had developed since they parted three days earlier.

This trooper could not have been Trumpeter Martin, who headed *south* with his message to Benteen, and it is known that trumpeters rode white (or grey) horses. Curly seems quite definite about the color of this man's horse, and there is an interesting statement made in Walter Camp's summary of his interview with Pvt. James Wilber of Company "M": "Wilber says Dick Hanley [a sergeant with "C" Company] told him that a C troop man left Custer later than Trumpeter Martin."[45]

Douglas Ellison, in his fascinating book, "Sole Survivor,"[46] believes that this trooper was Frank Finkel, who surfaced in Dayton, Washington, and told his story in 1921. Ellison makes an interesting and persuasive case for Finkel (who claimed to have been a member of Company "C"), and his book deserves a reading as a sidelight to the Custer Battle.

However, General Godfrey, in his narrative of the battle, speaks of the possibility of another survivor: "The question has often been asked if any soldier escaped. In August we camped at the mouth of the Rosebud where we found the carcass of a horse *shot in the head* [italics apparently Godfrey's]; near the horse was a carbine; on the saddle was a small grain sack made of canvas and used by the 7th Cavalry only to carry oats during the march, when detached from the wagons. At the time of the discovery we conjectured that some man had escaped, and on reaching the river had killed his horse for meat and used the saddle straps to tie together a raft. An Indian would not have left the carbine but the man may have abandoned it, either because he was out of ammunition or could not risk the extra weight on his raft."[47]

Walter Camp was apparently intrigued by this story, for he later asked others about it. Pvt. Jacob Adams of Company "H" told him: "After we left Pease Bottom, we camped on the north side of the Yellowstone, opposite the Rosebud. After we broke camp there I saw a dead soldier and dead horse south of the Yellowstone and within sight of the Yellowstone — only a few miles from it. The body was then thought to be one of L troop men who had been with Custer and scalped. The carbine was with the body and all equipment, and the leather sling was still over the shoulder. We concluded that both the man and the horse had been wounded and had gotten that far and given out."⁴⁸

Lieutenant Charles Roe of Gibbon's 2nd Cavalry said: "While lying in camp on the north side of the Yellowstone opposite the mouth of the Rosebud in August 1876, it was reported in Gibbon's camp that the body of a cavalry soldier and his horse were found on the south side of the Yellowstone, not far from that stream and not far from the Rosebud. At the time no one seemed to doubt the story, and it was commonly supposed to have been the remains of a man who escaped from the Custer fight." Roe went on to make it clear that this was not the body of one of their own men: "The bodies of the two soldiers of Gibbon's killed over there in the spring while hunting antelope had been recovered by a troop of cavalry at the time. [Pvts. Stoker and Raymier of Co. H, 2nd Cavalry, and James Quinn, a civilian, were killed by Indians on May 23, 1876, while hunting]."⁴⁹

Sergeant Daniel Kanipe of "C" Company, in a letter to Walter Camp on July 29, 1908, said, "The dead trooper with his gun and dead horse still lariated to the picket pin was found a few days' journey from Custer's hill. It was not six months before his body was found, but was somewheres about three or four weeks. General Cook's *[sic]* command found him. He was over in the Rose Bud country. He was in the direction of about east, or southeast [northeast?] from the battlefield where Custer was found. I knew the man well. His name was Short, but I do not remember his given name. He belonged to "C" Troop, my company. How I came to know it was Short of my company was that he had his stuff numbered 50, and General Crook reported that the man's number was 50. *He was with the company when I left it,* on Reno's hill."⁵⁰ (Italics mine, CdB.) Kanipe, it will be remembered, was the first messenger sent by Custer as the battalion reached the bluffs overlooking the river.

In another Camp interview, Pvt. George Glenn of Company "H" added a seemingly unrelated story: "On our way up the Rosebud to meet Crook, a cavalryman's hat was found near the Rosebud. I saw the hat. It was a white wool hat, with brass crossed sabers and the brass letter 'C.' It was passed around among the men to see if any could identify the owner of it."[51]

Kanipe tied it together in a letter to Camp in November 1909: "Short wore a light hat with the cross sabres drawn on the front of it with the number '7' between the sabres... It was a common thing for the men to mark their equipment with their initials for identification. There were very few men in the company who marked their hats as Short did, but I recall very well that he had marked his in this manner. The soldiers all had their hats marked but usually on the inside. I heard Nathan Short's body had been found after we marched from the mouth of the Big Horn to the Rosebud, but I did not see the remains. I only heard that the scouts had found them."[52]

Private Ferdinand Widmayer told Camp that "he saw Nathan Short. Heard that a dead soldier was found and went to see him. Bones of man and horse and carbine were found. Sling belt still on the skeleton. Says was near the Rosebud. Body lay out in open space near some brush but not in brush. No log near remains. A good many went to see it. Says body had been dead a long time and clothing rotted." Camp concluded these notes with the observation, "If this is correct could not have been Short, but he says the talk at the time was that it was supposed to have been one of Custer's men who got away. Says the remains of the man were buried there."[53]

Widmayer's reference to the "brush" must have been in response to a question by Camp based on what Colonel Richard Thompson of the 6th Infantry had told him in a previous interview. Camp's notes read: "Says he personally saw Nathan Short's horse and carbine but not the body of the man. They lay in some brush near Rosebud and Yellowstone, and at the time it was supposed that this man had escaped from the Custer fight. It is possible that by the time Thompson saw the horse, the remains of the man had been buried."[54]

Private Roman Rutten of Company "M'" said only that he, too, heard the Nathan Short story,[55] and Pvt. John McGuire of "C" Company told Camp that he "heard of Nathan Short. He got good distance toward Rosebud. Had bobtailed horse. Only bobtailed horse in Co. Had initials on cartridge belt."[56]

And finally, this brief note from Camp's interview with the scout, George Herendeen: "Nathan Short was found over on the Rosebud, pretty well down toward its mouth."[57]

As in most "eyewitness" testimony, there are variances in these accounts, yet there is a common thread running through all of them that gives credibility to the story. Only Adams said he saw the remains of both the man and the horse; Thompson and Godfrey saw only the horse, and Camp's surmise that by that time the body had been buried is probably the correct explanation. Glenn saw only the hat, but Kanipe, who did not see the body, did identify the hat as that of Short. The others only "heard" about the body, but the references to the fact that there was much talk among the men about it, suggests that perhaps a number of others, not interviewed by Camp, also saw the bodies of Short and his horse.

We can only guess how Nathan Short reached his final destination near the mouth of the Rosebud, 65 miles "as the crow flies" from the Custer Battlefield. He may have been the messenger of Curly's story, or he may have been one of those troopers described by the Indians as escaping from the field of battle, some of whom were "presumed" to have been caught and killed. Wooden Leg describes one such instance:

"A soldier on a horse suddenly appeared in view back behind the warriors who were coming from the eastward along the ridge. He was riding away to the eastward, as fast as he could make his horse go. It seemed he must have been hidden somewhere back there until the Indians had passed him. A band of the Indians, all of them Sioux, I believe, got after him. I lost sight of them when they went beyond a curve of the hilltop. I suppose, though, they caught him and killed him."[58]

What happened to Nathan Short? How did he die? We can't answer that; he, too is part of the Mystery.

EPILOGUE

The account of the Custer Battle we have presented is, as stated, one possible scenario of "What" occurred at the Little Big Horn and "How" it happened. We turn now to an evaluation of the circumstances which brought this military action to its tragic conclusion and will try to answer the remaining question: "Why?"

This is a question of judgment, of course, but judgment is not synonymous with condemnation. In a court of law we are brought to judgment, but under the presumption of "innocence until proven guilty." Judgment is the means of determining accountability, and the verdict — whether "guilty" or "innocent" — requires the unanimous agreement of the jury, after considering all the available evidence. Let us, then, examine that evidence, and without passion, try to render a verdict, realizing in advance that no matter what that verdict will be, it will not be unanimous!

The Expedition of 1876 as related here, was doomed from the start. Colonel Reynolds' attack upon the Cheyennes on Powder River contributed nothing positive, and the same can be said for General Crook's engagement at the Big Bend of the Rosebud. Yet even before these troops took to the field, the groundwork for eventual failure had already been laid. The dishonesty of some of the Indian agents in reporting fewer than the actual number of Indians absent from their reservations was critical, and resulted from a corrupt policy of appointing these representatives of the government as political "plums."

By reporting fewer absentees, the agents would continue to receive the largesse of the government for the larger number of Indians *supposed* to be present. The surplus could then be sold with the proceeds lining the pockets of the agents. Consequently, the totals given to the War Department by the Indian Bureau represented only a fraction of the actual number of those Indians then declared "hostiles."[1] Added to this was the lack of communication once the troops were in the field. Sheridan learned that the original total of absentees of 500 to 800 Indians was far too low, but by the time he learned it, it was too late to communicate the information to the troops in the field. As Edgerly said, at the time of the battle "General Sheridan knew that Sitting Bull's camp had been reinforced by 1,800 lodges... and we had received no intimation of it, and this is the principal reason for the disaster. We were marching to attack from 2,500 to 3,000 men, believing we had less than one-third of that number to fight."[2]

Early in the regiment's march up the Rosebud, Custer's examination of the trail led him to believe that the number of Indians now exceeded Sheridan's modest estimate, and Godfrey tells us that at the first night's bivouac, June 22, Custer shared his belief that "judging from the number of lodge-fires reported by Reno, that we might meet at least a thousand warriors; there might be enough young men from the agencies, visiting their hostile friends, to make a total of fifteen hundred."[3] Even this estimate turned out to be less than half of the actual number of hostile warriors.

The lack of communication existed on all levels. Crook's failure to inform Terry of his own encounter with the Indians on the Rosebud a week earlier was a critical omission. Had he sent messengers north to the Yellowstone with this information,

Terry would never have carried through his eventual battle plan. It must also be repeated that Crook's command, larger than Custer's and Gibbon's together, could have continued marching north along the Rosebud with no difficulty, and even after sending his wounded back to his Goose Creek camp, he could have met Custer near the mouth of Davis Creek in time to join forces with him.

We come now to a consideration of Custer's strategy. His division of the command into four components under Reno, Benteen, McDougall and the Keogh-Yates battalions which he accompanied, has drawn both criticism and praise. Of the officers present on the Little Big Horn, Benteen, Hare and Moylan (among others) blamed the disaster on the division of the regiment. In a letter to Goldin, Benteen attributed the defeat to "the regiment being broken up into four columns, and none of the four within supporting distance of either of the others, (without any orders even to be such a support to any...) That is all I blame Custer for — the scattering, as it were, (two portions of his command, anyway) to the — well, four winds, before he knew anything about the exact or approximate position of the Indian village or the Indians."[4]

Walter Camp told Colonel Graham that in an interview he had with Lt. Hare, the lieutenant said that "In his opinion General Custer was to blame for the entire disaster."[5]

As a footnote to his reprint of Godfrey's narrative of the battle, Graham said that in the original version of 1892, Godfrey wrote: "A number of officers collected on the edge of the bluff overlooking the valley and were discussing the situation: among our number was Captain Moylan, a veteran soldier and a good one too, watching the scene below." (This was after Benteen joined Reno on the hill, ed.) "Moylan remarked quite emphatically, 'Gentlemen, in my opinion General Custer has made the biggest mistake in his life, by not taking the whole regiment in at once in the first attack.'"[6]

This, of course, was not Godfrey's opinion; in summing up the causes of the defeat Godfrey wrote: "The division of the command was not in itself faulty. The same tactics were pursued at the battle of Washita and were successful. That was a surprise attack and there was *full co-operation* (italics are Godfrey's) of the separate commands, each commander carried out his instructions."

Godfrey went on to say that if Reno had "made his charge as ordered, or made a bold front even, the Hostiles would have been so engaged in the bottom that Custer's approach from the Northeast would have been such a surprise as to cause the stampede of the village and would have broken the morale of the warriors."[7]

Edgerly agreed with this assessment with a qualification: "I believe (Custer) fully intended charging in rear of and in support of Reno, but when he saw how fordable the stream was and what little resistance Reno was making, he determined to move down that stream to the village, then in plain view, strike it in the flank, and he undoubtedly expected to meet the victorious Reno in the middle of the Village. This don't *[sic]* appear to me to be bad tactics, and if his orders to Reno had been carried out and there had not been more than 800 Indians, the plan would have undoubtedly succeeded."[8]

These references to Reno's fight in the valley require us to review that action. Although this battle was Reno's first experience at fighting Indians, his Civil War record was an honorable one. He was brevetted repeatedly for gallantry in action, yet his indecision in the valley fight, and his failure to hold a position there — continuing to engage the hostiles and threaten the village, if not by aggressive action, then at least by his presence alone — was perhaps the major contributory factor in releasing a number of warriors to concentrate on Custer and foil his attempt to strike the Indians from the north while Reno engaged them from the south. Had Reno held his position in the timber, he would certainly have occupied the Indians and Custer would have been able to get into position.

It was not cowardice that prompted Reno to retreat so ignominiously, but rather momentary panic, and that panic destroyed the discipline of his command. Reno's later attempt to justify his actions by describing the timber position as being untenable was not supported by others. Benteen said it was a "number one place," and that it was a great deal better than the hilltop position. General Gibbon and Lt. Godfrey agreed, as did Lts. DeRudio and Hare, both of whom were in the valley fight with Reno. The Arickara interpreter, Fred Gerard, summed up his own feelings in an interview with Walter Camp in 1909: "It occurred to me then, and I am still of the same opinion, that this timber was a splendid place for defense, and that Reno made a terrible blunder in not remaining right there. The Sioux were thick enough outside, mostly at long range, however; but had a determination been displayed in the way of defense, they would never have come into the brush to find the soldiers. It is certain that if Reno had held out against these Indians, hundreds of them would have remained to hold him in the timber, and Custer would have had a better show at the other end of the village."[9]

In Godfrey's comparison of this battle with Custer's victory at the Washita, he makes the point that the Washita "was a surprise attack and there was full co-operation of the separate commands, each commander carried out his instructions." He was speaking of Reno's failure to hold his position in the timber, but the charge may also be leveled at the other battalion commanders. McDougall, of course, had a comparatively easy assignment: to guard the packtrain, and this he did in good order. We cannot, of course, judge the actions of Keogh and Yates for we do not know what their orders were, but we can challenge Benteen's compliance with his instructions, both oral and written.

Sending Benteen on a scouting mission to the left from the divide was necessary if Custer was to determine the location of the Indians more precisely. Although Custer never received this information from Benteen, it is probable that he was able to determine it himself when he neared the river and was able to see that there were no Indians to the south. As it developed, Benteen's scout was, as he insisted on calling it, "senseless," but at the time he was sent on his scout its purpose was essential. The information Custer received from Gerard, that the Indians were "running away," required an immediate response, and sending Reno's battalion to harass them from the rear in order to slow down their retreat was the only logical tactic to employ. Had the Indians really been trying to escape, this maneuver would surely have achieved its objective and Custer would have had ample time to head them off as he attempted to do.

Benteen stated that his orders were "to move to the left to a line of bluffs about 2 miles away. Sending out an officer and a few men as advance guard, to 'pitch in' to anything I came across, and to notify him (Custer) at once." Although it is obvious that Benteen made only a token attempt at carrying out these orders, going but a short distance to the left before turning back to the main trail, the result had no effect on the outcome of the battle. It was the "long time" spent at the morass which Godfrey described as causing concern among the officers that we find inexcusable, for had Benteen kept that halt brief, he would have been close on the heels of Custer and would probably have joined him. As for Benteen's failure to obey the direct written order of Custer to "Come on, be quick, bring packs," we have no explanation. The extraordinary delay in moving from Reno Hill to "the sound of the guns" is equally inexplicable, for that was part of the soldier's "code of honor." Although Reno was the ranking officer, nevertheless it was Benteen whom Custer had specifically ordered to join him, and once order had been restored to Reno's command, there was no further excuse for remaining there for another hour and a half after the packtrain arrived. The ammunition packs could have been cut out of the train and Benteen could have delivered them to Custer while he waited on Nye-Cartwright Ridge.

The wisdom which seems to accrue from hindsight forces us to agree that the division of the regiment was a fatal error. Yet to say this is to imply that Custer had a more reasonable option which he rejected in favor of this one, when in fact he acted upon the only information available to him by his scouts — information that was totally false. What was said in defense of Reno in Chapter Five might also be said in Custer's defense: that he made a judgment call, "one which a commander must be expected to make on the basis of his assessment of the situation, and whether it was a wise decision or a tactical error could not be known at the time it was made. This is the kind of dilemma faced by military leaders in circumstances that demand an instant determination of what course must be followed, and will inevitably be subject to the scrutiny of hindsight."

On Nye-Cartwright Ridge, Custer waited in vain for some indication that Benteen was on his way. When he realized that no help was forthcoming, he had to make a decision: to proceed with the forces available, or to retreat. A lesser man — perhaps even a more prudent man — might have done the latter, but to retreat in the face of the enemy was contrary to Custer's nature, and having revealed his presence on the heights above the Little Big Horn, he must have known the futility of such an action. Only bold action could now save his command, and that is the course he chose. We may call it the result of foolish pride or an inordinate overconfidence in his beloved 7th, or we may call it simply courage.

When all the evidence is weighed and the actions of all the participants have been reviewed, there remains the one, final and indisputable observation that must be confronted. It was voiced long ago by another great Indian fighter, General Nelson A. Miles: "No commanding officer can win victories with seven-twelfths of his command remaining out of the engagement when within the sound of his rifle-shots."[10]

ROSTER

Roster of
The 7th U.S. Cavalry Regiment
June, 1876

Key to Symbols:
* * indicates did not participate in the battle, June 25-26, 1876. (Includes those on detached service, absent on leave, absent without leave (AWOL), absent on sick leave.
* † indicates wounded in action, June 25-26.
* ‡ indicates killed in action, June 25-26. When name is *followed* by (‡ and date), indicates soldier died later of wounds.
* aka indicates the soldier was also known by an alias.
* KWC Killed with Custer battalion.
* KIV Killed in the valley fight with Reno battalion.
* KOH Killed on (Reno) Hill with Reno-Benteen battalions.

"Rank" is regular army rank at time of battle; "Unit" refers to regular company assignment (when followed by (w/L, for example, this means the soldier was temporarily on duty with Co. L; "w/A" means on duty with Co. A, etc.)

Officers names are in **bold face.**

NAME	RANK	UNIT
Abbotts, Harry	Pvt.	E
*Abos, James A.	Pvt.	B
Abrams, William G.	Pvt.	L
*Ackerman, Charles	Pvt.	K
*Ackison, David	Pvt.	E
‡Adams, George E.	Pvt.	L (KWC)
Adams, Jacob	Pvt.	H
Akers, James (Sgt. 6/25)	Cpl.	G
Alberts, James H.	Pvt.	D
*Alcott, Samuel	Sgt.	A
‡Allan, Fred C.	Pvt.	C (KWC)
Aller, Charles	Pvt.	A
Allerton, Benjamin F.	Pvt.	L
*Anderson, Charles L.	Pvt.	C
*Anderson, George	Pvt.	K
‡Andrews, William	Pvt.	L (KWC)
‡Armstrong, John E.	Pvt.	A (KIV)
*Arndt, Otto	Pvt.	Band
*Arnold, Herbert	Blksmth	C
Ascough, John B.	Pvt.	D
‡Assadaly, Anthony	Pvt.	L (KWC)
‡Atchison, Thomas	Pvt.	F (KWC)
*Avery, Charles E.	Pvt.	H
‡Babcock, Elmer	Pvt.	L (KWC)
‡Bailey, Henry A.	Saddler	I (KWC)
Bailey, John A.	Saddler	B
‡Baker, William H.	Pvt.	E (KWC)
*Bammbach, Conrad	Pvt.	Band
Bancroft, Neil	Pvt.	A
Banet, Thomas K.	Pvt.	L
*Barnet, Charles	Pvt.	G
‡Barry, John	Pvt.	I (KWC)
Barry, Peter O.	Pvt.	B
Barsantee, James F.	Pvt.	B

ROSTER

‡Barth, Robert	Pvt.	E (KWC)
Bates, Joseph	Pvt.	M
*Bauer, Jacob	Pvt.	K
Baumgartner, Louis	Pvt.	A
*Beck, Benjamin	Pvt.	Band
Bell, James E.	1st Lt.	D
*Bender, Henry	Sgt.	L
†Bennett, James C.	Pvt.	C (‡7/6)
Benteen, Frederick W.	Capt.	H
Berwold, Frank	Pvt.	E
*Bischoff, Charles H.	Pvt.	C
Bishley, Henry	Pvt.	H
†Bishop, Alexander B.	Cpl.	H
†Bishop, Charles H.	Pvt.	H
†Black, Henry	Pvt.	H
*Blair, James C.	Pvt.	K
Blair, Wilbur F.	Pvt.	A
Blake, Thomas	Pvt.	A
Blunt, George	Pvt.	K
Boam, William	Pvt.	B
‡Bobo, Edwin	1st Sgt.	C (KWC)
*Bockerman, August	Pvt.	A
Boggs, James	Pvt.	F
Boissen, Christian	Saddler	K
*Bonner, Hugh	Pvt.	B
Boren, Ansgarius	Pvt.	B
Bott, George	Pvt.	A
‡Botzer, Edward	Sgt.	G (KIV)
*Bowers, Frank	Pvt.	M
Boyle, James J.	Pvt.	G
‡Boyle, Owen	Pvt.	E (KWC)
Braden, Charles	1st Lt.	L
‡Brady, William	Pvt.	F (KWC)
Brainerd, George	Pvt.	B
*Brandle, William	Pvt.	C
‡Brandon, Benjamin	Farrier	F (KWC)
Brant, Abraham	Pvt.	D
†Braun, Frank	Pvt.	M (‡10/4)
Brennan, John	Pvt.	C

Bresnahan, Cornelius	Pvt.	K
‡Brightfield, John	Pvt.	C (KWC)
Bringes, John	Farrier	A
Brinkerhoff, Henry	Pvt.	G (Cpl. 6/25)
‡Briody, John	Cpl.	F (KWC)
‡Broadhurst, Joseph	Pvt.	I (KWC)
‡Brogan, James	Pvt.	E (KWC)
Brown, Alexander	Sgt.	G
‡Brown, Benjamin F.	Pvt.	F (KWC)
*Brown, Charles	Sgt.	HQ
‡Brown, George C.	Cpl.	E (KWC)
Brown, Henry	Pvt.	I
*Brown, Hiram E.	Pvt.	F
*Brown, James	Pvt.	B
Brown, Joseph	Pvt.	K
‡Brown, William	Pvt.	F (KWC)
Brownnell, Latrobe	Pvt.	E
‡Bruce, Patrick	Pvt.	F (KWC)
*Bruns, August	Pvt.	E
‡Bucknell, Thomas J.	Trmptr.	C (KWC)
*Burdick, Benjamin F.	Pvt.	A
*Burgdorf, Charles J.	Pvt.	K
Burkhardt, Charles	Pvt.	K
Burke, Edmund H.	Blksmth	K
‡Burke, John	Pvt.	L (KWC)
Burkman, John	Pvt.	L
*Burlis, Edward	Pvt.	Band
‡Burnham, Lucien	Pvt.	F (KWC)
*Burns, Charles	Pvt.	B
‡Bustard, James	Sgt.	I (KWC)
‡Butler, James	1st Sgt.	L (KWC)
Butler, John	Pvt.	F
*Caddle, Michael	Sgt.	I
Cain, Morris	Pvt.	M
*Caldwell, William M.	Pvt.	B
‡**Calhoun, James**	1st Lt.	C (w/L-KWC)
‡Callahan, John J.	Cpl.	K (KWC)
*Callan, James	Pvt.	B
Callan, Thomas J.	Pvt.	B

Campbell, Charles A.	Pvt.	B
†Campbell, Charles	Pvt.	G
Campbell, Jeremiah	Sgt.	K
*Capes, William	Sgt.	M
†Carey, Patrick	Sgt.	M
Carmody, Thomas	Pvt.	B
‡Carney, James	Pvt.	F (KWC)
*Carroll, Daniel	Sgt.	B
*Carroll, Joseph	Pvt.	Band
*Carter, Andrew	Pvt.	Band
*Carter, Cassius R.	Trmptr.	G
Casey, John J.	Pvt.	B
‡Cashan, William	Sgt.	L (KWC)
‡Cather, Armantheus	Pvt.	F (KWC)
*Causby, Thomas	QM Sgt.	HQ
*Centan, Thomas	Pvt.	D
Channell, William	Pvt.	H
‡Charley, Vincent	Farrier	D (KOH)
(on monument: "Charley Vincent")		
‡Cheever, Ami	Pvt.	L (KWC)
Chesterwood, Charles	Pvt.	K
(aka "John C. Creighton")		
Churchill, F.F.	Civ.	Packer
Clark, Frank	Pvt.	B
‡Clear, Elihu F.	Pvt.	K (KIV)
Coakley, Patrick	Pvt.	K
Cody, Henry (*See:* Scollin, Henry M.)		
‡Coleman, Charles	Cpl.	F (KWC)
Coleman, Thomas W.	Pvt.	B
*Colwell, John R.	Pvt.	L
*Conlan, Michael	Pvt.	L
*Conlon, Thomas	Pvt.	D
*Connell, John	Trmptr.	B
Connelly, Patrick	Sgt.	H
‡Conner, Edward	Pvt.	E (KWC)
‡Conners, Thomas	Pvt.	I (KWC)
Connor, Andrew	Pvt.	A
‡Considine, Martin	Sgt.	G (KIV)
‡**Cooke, William W.**	1st Lt.	HQ (KWC)

Cookey, Benjamin R.	Pvt.	E
†Cooney, David (Sgt. 6/28)	Pvt.	I (‡7/20)
†Cooper, John	Pvt.	H
*Corcoran, John	Pvt.	C
†Corcoran, Patrick	Pvt.	K
*Corwine, Richard W.	Pvt.	A
Cowley, Cornelius	Pvt.	A
*Cowley, Stephen	Pvt.	D
Cox, Thomas	Pvt.	D
*Crandall, Charles A.	Cpl.	C
Cranston, Robert	Pvt.	I
*Crawford, William L.	Pvt.	K
Craycroft, William T.	1st Lt.	B
Creighton, John C. (*See:* Chesterwood)		
*Cressey, Melancthon H.	Cpl.	G
‡Criddle, Christopher	Pvt.	C (KWC)
‡Crisfield, William B.	Pvt.	L (KWC)
†Criswell, Benjamin	Sgt.	B
Criswell, Harry	Pvt.	B
‡**Crittenden, John J.**	2nd Lt.	w/L (KWC)
Crowe, Michael	Pvt.	B
Crowley, Patrick	Pvt.	B
Crump, John	Blksmth.	B
Culbertson, Ferdinand	Sgt.	A
*Cunningham, Albert J.	Cpl.	D
†Cunningham, Charles	Cpl.	B
Curtis, William A.	Sgt.	E
‡Custer, Boston	Civ.	Packer (KWC)
‡**Custer, George A.**	Lt. Col.	HQ (KWC)
‡**Custer, Thomas W.**	Capt.	C (KWC)
‡Dalious, James	Cpl.	A (KIV)
Dann, George	Pvt.	D
‡Darris, John	Pvt.	E (KWC)
Davenport, William H.	Pvt.	B
Davern, Edward (Sgt. 6/25)	Pvt.	F
Davis, Harrison	Pvt.	M
‡Davis, William	Pvt.	E (KWC)
Dawsey, David E.	Pvt.	D

Day, John	Pvt.	H
Deitline, Frederick	Blksmth.	D
*Delaney, Michael	Pvt.	K
Denny, George W.	Pvt.	F
De Rudio, Charles C.	1st Lt.	E (w/A)
*De Tourriel, Louis	Pvt.	B
Devoto, Augustus L.	Pvt.	B
Dewey, George W.	Pvt.	H
‡**De Wolf, J.M.**	Ass't. Surg.	HQ (KIV)
Diamond, Edward	Pvt.	H
†Diehle, Jacob	Pvt.	A
‡Dohman, Anton	Pvt.	F (KWC)
*Dolan, John	Pvt.	M
*Doll, Jacob W.	Pvt.	B
Donahue, John 1st	Saddler	M
Donahue, John 2nd	Pvt.	K
‡Donnelly, Timothy	Pvt.	F (KWC)
*Dooley, Patrick	Pvt.	K
‡Dorman, Isaiah	Civ. Intrptr.	(KIV)
‡Dorn, Richard	Pvt.	B (KOH)
‡Dose, Henry	Trmptr.	G (KWC)
Dougherty, James	Cpl.	B
*Downing, Alexander	Pvt.	F
‡Downing, Thomas P.	Pvt.	I (KWC)
*Drago, Henry	Sgt.	F
‡Drinan, James	Pvt.	A (KIV)
‡Driscoll, Edward	Pvt.	I (KWC)
‡Duggan, John	Pvt.	L (KWC)
Durselen, Otto (aka "Otto Durselow)	Pvt.	A
Dwyer, Edmund	Pvt.	G
‡Dye, William	Pvt.	L (KWC)
*Eades, William	Pvt.	F
‡Eagan, Thomas P. (aka "Thomas Hagan")	Cpl.	E (KWC)
Easley, John T.	Sgt.	A
*Eckerson, E.P.	2nd Lt.	L
Edgerly, Winfield S.	2nd Lt.	D

*Eininberger, Peter	Pvt.	Band
‡Eisemann, George	Pvt.	C (KWC)
*Emerich, Jacob	Pvt.	Band
‡Engle, Gustave	Pvt.	C (KWC)
Etzler, William	Pvt.	L
†Fahl, John	Sgt.	H
*Farber, Conrad	Pvt.	I
†Farley, William	Pvt.	H
‡Farrand, James	Pvt.	C (KWC)
‡Farrell, Richard	Pvt.	E (KWC)
Farrer, Morris	Pvt.	C
Fay, John J.	Pvt.	D
Fehler, Henry	Sgt.	A
‡Finckle, August	Sgt.	C (KWC)
*Findersen, Hugo	Sgt.	L
‡Finley, Jeremiah	Sgt.	C (KWC)
*Fisher, Charles 1st	Sgt.	K
Fisher, Charles 2nd	Trmptr	M
Fitzgerald, John	Farrier	C
Flanagan, James	Sgt.	D
*Flood, Phillip	Pvt.	G
‡Foley, John 1st	Cpl.	C (KWC)
Foley, John 2nd	Pvt.	K
†Foster, Samuel	Pvt.	A
Fowler, Isaac	Pvt.	C
*Fox, Frederick	Pvt.	I
*Fox, Harry A.	Pvt.	D
Fox, John	Pvt.	D
Frank, William	Pvt.	B
Franklin, John W.	Pvt.	A
Frederick, Andrew	Sgt.	K
‡French, Henry E.	Cpl.	C (KWC)
French, Thomas H.	Capt.	M
Frett, John	Civ.	Packer
*Gaffney, George	Sgt.	I

Gallene, Jean B.D.	Pvt.	M
‡Galvan, James J.	Pvt.	L (KWC)
*Gannon, Peter	Sgt.	B
‡Gardiner, William	Pvt.	F (KWC)
*Garlick, Edward	1st Sgt.	G
Garlington, E.A.	2nd Lt.	H
*Geesbacher, Gabriel	Pvt.	I
*Gehrmann, Frederick	Pvt.	B
Geiger, George	Sgt.	H
*Geist, Frank J.	Pvt.	G
†George, William	Pvt.	H (‡7/3)
Gibbs, William	Pvt.	K
Gibson, Frank M.	1st Lt.	H
Gilbert, John M.	Pvt.	A
*Gilbert, Julius	Pvt.	E
‡Gilbert, William H.	Cpl.	L (KWC)
‡Gillette, David C.	Pvt.	I (KWC)
Girard (Gerard), Fred	Civ.	Intrptr.
Glenn, George W. (aka "George W. Glease)	Pvt.	H
Godfrey, Edward S.	1st Lt.	K
Golden, Bernard	Pvt.	M
‡Golden, Patrick	Pvt.	D (KOH)
Goldin, Theodore	Pvt.	H
‡Gordon, Henry	Pvt.	M (KIV)
Gordon, Thomas A.	Pvt.	K
‡Graham, Charles	Pvt.	L (KWC)
Graham, Thomas	Pvt.	G
*Gray, John	Pvt.	B
*Gray, William S.	Pvt.	G
Grayson, Edward	Pvt.	G
*Green, John	Pvt.	D
Green, Joseph	Pvt.	D
*Greene, Thomas	Pvt.	K
*Griesner, Julius	Pvt.	Band
‡Griffin, Patrick	Pvt.	C (KWC)
*Grimes, Andrew	Pvt.	I

‡Gross, George H.	Pvt.	I (KWC)
*Gunther, Julius	Pvt.	K
*Gust, Frank J.	Pvt.	G
*Haack, Charles L.	Pvt.	I
Hackett, John	Pvt.	G
Hagan, Thomas (*See:* Eagan, Thomas P.)		
‡Hagemann, Otto	Cpl.	G (KIV)
Hale, Owen	Capt.	K
Haley, Timothy	Pvt.	H
Hall, Curtis	Pvt.	D
*Hall, Edward	Pvt.	D
Hamilton, Andrew	Blksmth.	A
‡Hamilton, Henry	Pvt.	L (KWC)
Hammon, John E.	Cpl.	G (Sgt. 6/25)
‡Hammond, George W.	Pt.	F (KWC)
Hanley, Richard P.	Sgt.	C
Hardow, Robert	Pvt.	C
Hardy, William G.	Trmptr.	A
Hare, Luther R.	2nd Lt.	K
*Harlfinger, Gustave	Pvt.	D
Harrden, William	Pvt.	D
‡**Harrington, Henry M.**	2nd Lt.	C (KWC)
‡Harrington, Weston	Pvt.	L (KWC)
Harris, David W.	Pvt.	A
Harris, James	Pvt.	D
*Harris, Leonard A.	Pvt.	F
Harris, William M.	Pvt.	D
Harrison, Thomas W.	Sgt.	D
‡Harrison, William H.	Cpl.	L (KWC)
Harrold, William M.	Pvt.	F
Hasck, Henry	Pvt.	H
‡Hathersall, James	Pvt.	C (KWC)
Hauck, August A.	Pvt.	F
‡Haugge, Louis	Pvt.	L (KWC)
‡Hawell, George	Saddler	C (KWC)
Hayer, John	Pvt.	D

*Haywood, George	Pvt.	I
‡Heath, William H.	Farrier	L (KWC)
Hedison, James	Pvt.	G
*Hegner, Francis	Pvt.	F
Heid, George	Pvt.	M
‡Heim, John	Pvt.	E (KWC)
‡Helmer, Julius	Pvt.	K (KOH)
*Henderson, George W.	Pvt.	G
‡Henderson, John	Pvt.	E (KWC)
‡Henderson, Sykes	Pvt.	E (KWC)
Herendeen, George	Civ.	Scout
‡Hetismer, Adam	Pvt.	I (KWC)
†Hetler, Jacob	Pvt.	D
†Heyn, William	1st Sgt.	A
‡Hieber, William	Pvt.	E (KWC)
‡Hiley, John	Pvt.	E (KWC)
Hill, James	1st Sgt.	B
‡**Hodgson, Benjamin H.**	2nd Lt.	B (KIV)
*Hoehn, Max	Pvt.	L
‡Hohmeyer, Frederick	1st Sgt.	E (KWC)
‡Holcomb, Edward P.	Pvt.	I (KWC)
Holden, Henry	Pvt.	D
*Holihan, Andrew	Pvt.	K
†Holmstead, Frederick	Pvt.	A
*Hood, Charles M.	Pvt.	H
Hook, Stanton	Pvt.	A
Horn, George	Pvt.	D
‡Horn, Marion E.	pvt.	I (KWC)
*Horner, Jacob	Pvt.	K
Hose, George (Sgt. 6.26)	Cpl.	K
*Houghtaling, Charles H.	Pvt.	D
‡Housen, Edward	Pvt.	D (KOH)
*Howard, Frank	Pvt.	E
*Hoyt, Walter	Pvt.	K
‡Hughes, Francis T.	Pvt.	L (KWC)
‡Hughes, Robert	Sgt.	K (KWC)
Hughes, Thomas	Pvt.	H
Hunt, George	Pvt.	D

Hunt, John	Pvt.	H
Hunter, Frank	Farrier	F
Hurel, James	Pvt.	D
Hutchinson, Rufus	Sgt.	B
*Hutter, Anton	Pvt.	E
*Ilsley, Charles S.	Capt.	E
Ionson, Emil O.	Pvt.	A
*Jackson, Henry	1st Lt.	F
‡James, William B.	Sgt.	E (KWC)
Jenneys, Alonzo	Pvt.	K
Johnson, Benjamin	Pvt.	G
Johnson, Samuel	Pvt.	A
Johnston, Francis (*See:* Kennedy, F.J.)		
‡Jones, Julien D.	Pvt.	H (KOH)
Jordan, John	Pvt.	C
*Jungbluth, Julius	Pvt.	Band
*Kane, William	Pvt.	C
Kanipe, Daniel A.	Sgt.	C
*Katzenmaier, Jacob	Pvt.	G
Kavanagh, John	Pvt.	D
‡Kavanagh, Thomas	Pvt.	L (KWC)
Kavannagh, Charles	Pvt.	M
*Keefe, John J.	Pvt.	B
*Keegan, Michael	Pvt.	L
Keller, John	Pvt.	D
‡Kelley, Patrick	Pvt.	I (KWC)
‡Kellogg, Mark	Civ.	Corresp. (KWC)
Kelly, George	Pvt.	H
Kelly, Jack	Pvt.	L
Kelly, James 1st	Pvt.	H
Kelly, James 2nd	Trmptr	B
‡Kelly, John	Pvt.	F (KWC)
Kennedy, Francis J. (aka "Francis Johnston")	Pvt.	I
‡Kenny, Michael	1st Sgt.	F (KWC)
‡Keogh, Myles W.	Capt.	I (KWC)

*Kerr, Dennis	Pvt.	A
*Kilfoyle, Martin	Pvt.	G
†King, George H.	Cpl.	A (‡7/2)
‡King, John	Farrier	C (KWC)
Kipp, Fremont	Pvt.	D
*Klaweiter, Ferdinand	Pvt.	B
‡Klein, Gustave	Pvt.	F (KWC)
*Klein, Nikolaus	Pvt.	F
‡Klotzbucher, Henry	Pvt.	M (KIV)
‡Knauth, Herman	Pvt.	F (KWC)
‡Knecht, Andy	Pvt.	E (KWC)
*Kneubuchler, Joseph	Pvt.	Band
Korn, Gustave	Blksmth.	I
‡Kramer, William	Trmptr.	C (KWC)
Kretchmer, Joseph	Pvt.	D
*Kuehl, Jesse	Pvt.	D
Lacey, Michael J.	Pvt.	F
*Laden, Joseph	Pvt.	G
Lalor, William	Cpl.	M
Lamb, John	Pvt.	E
*Lambertin, Frank	Pvt.	H
Larned, Charles W.	2nd Lt.	F
Larrabee, William H.	Pvt.	L
Lasley, William W.	Pvt.	K
Lattman, John	Pvt.	G
*Lauper, Frank	Pvt.	G
Lawhorn, Thomas	Pvt.	H
*Lawler, James	Pvt.	G
Lebeldy, Anthony	Pvt.	F
*Lee, Mark E.	Pvt.	I
Lefler, Meier	Pvt.	F
‡Lehman, Frederick	Pvt.	I (KWC)
‡Lehman, Henry	Pvt.	I (KWC)
‡Lell, George	Cpl.	H (KOH)
*Lepper, Frederick	Pvt.	L
‡Lerock, William	Pvt.	F (KWC)
*Lewis, David W.	Pvt.	B
‡Lewis, John	Pvt.	C (KWC)

*Lewis, Uriah S.	Pvt.	D
‡Liddiard, Herod T.	Pvt.	E (KOH)
*Lieberman, Andrew	Pvt.	K
‡Lieman, Werner L.	Pvt.	F (KWC)
*Littlefield, John L.	Pvt.	B
‡Lloyd, Edward W.	Pvt.	I (KWC)
*Lloyd, Frank	Sgt.	G
‡Lobering, Louis	Pvt.	L (KWC)
*Lombard, Frank	Pvt.	Band
‡Lord, George E.	Ass't. Surg.	HQ (KWC)
‡Lorentz, George	Pvt.	M (KIV)
‡Lossee, William A.	Pvt.	F (KWC)
*Lovett, Meridith	Pvt.	C
Loyd, George (Cpl. 6/25)	Pvt.	G
Lynch, Dennis	Pvt.	F
*Lynch, Patrick	Pvt.	I
Lyons, Bernard	Pvt.	F
*Lyons, Daniel	Pvt.	K
‡Mack, George B.	Pvt.	B (KIV)
†Madden, Michael P. (Sgt. 6/26)	Pvt.	K
‡Madson, Christian	Pvt.	F (KWC)
‡Mahoney, Berthol	Pvt.	L (KWC)
Mahoney, Daniel	Pvt.	M
Mahoney, John	Pvt.	C
Mahoney, Thomas	Pvt.	C
†Maller, Jan	Pvt.	H
‡Mann, Frank C.	Civ.	Packer (KOH)
Manning, Davis	Pvt.	D
‡Manning, James R.	Blksmth.	F (KWC)
Maroney, Matthew	Sgt.	H
†Marshall, Jasper	Pvt.	L
*Marshall, John M.	Farrier	H
Marshall, William A.	Pvt.	D
‡Martin, James	Cpl.	G (KIV)
Martin, John	Trmptr.	H
Martin, Michael	1st Sgt.	D
Martin, William	Pvt.	B
‡Mason, Henry S.	Cpl.	E (KWC)

Mathey, Edward G.	1st Lt.	M (w/B)
‡Maxwell, Thomas E.	Pvt.	L (KWC)
McCabe, John	Pvt.	B
*McCall, Joseph	Cpl.	I
*McCann, Patrick	Pvt.	E
‡McCarthy, Charles	Pvt.	L (KWC)
McClurg, William	Pvt.	A
*McConnell, James	Pvt.	M
McConnell, Wilson	Pvt.	K
McCormick, Samuel	Pvt.	G
*McCreedy, Thomas	Cpl.	C
McCue, Martin	Pvt.	K
McCurry, Joseph	1st Sgt.	H
McDermott, George	Sgt.	A
McDermott, Thomas	Pvt.	H
‡McDonald, James	Pvt.	A (KIV)
McDonnell, John	Pvt.	G
†McDonnell, Patrick	Pvt.	D
*McDonough, James	Pvt.	G
McDougall, Thomas	Capt.	B
McEagen, John	Pvt.	G
‡McElroy, Thomas	Trmptr.	E (KWC)
‡McGinnes, John J.	Pvt.	G (KIV)
McGlone, John	Sgt.	M
McGonigle, Hugh	Pvt.	G
‡McGucker, John	Trmptr.	I (KWC)
‡McGue, Peter	Pvt.	L (KWC)
*McGuinniss, John	Pvt.	I
†McGuire, John	Pvt.	C
*McGurn, Bernard	Pvt.	B
‡McIlhargey, Archibald	Pvt.	I (KWC)
‡**McIntosh, Donald**	1st Lt.	G (KIV)
*McKay, Edward J.	Pvt.	G
*McKee, John	Pvt.	G
McLaughlin, Terrence	Pvt.	B
McLaughlin, Thomas	Sgt.	H
McMasters, William	Pvt.	B
McNamara, James	Pvt.	H
*McPeak, Alexander	Pvt.	L

McShane, John	Sgt.	I
†McVay, John	Pvt.	G
McVeigh, David	Trmptr.	A
*McWilliams, David	Pvt.	H
‡Meador, Thomas E.	Pvt.	H (KOH)
Meadville, J.R. (aka "John Meadwell")	Pvt.	D
Mecklin, Henry W.B.	Blksmth.	H
†Meier, John H.	Pvt.	M
*Meinike, Ernst	Saddler	F
Merrill, Lewis	Major	HQ
*Merritt, George A.	Pvt.	Band
‡Meyer, Albert H.	Cpl.	E (KWC)
‡Meyer, August	Pvt.	C (KWC)
‡Meyer, Frederick	Pvt.	C (KWC)
‡Meyer, William D.	Pvt.	M (KIV)
Meyers, John	Saddler	D
†Mielke, Max	Pvt.	K
Miles, James	Pvt.	L
*Miller, Edwin	Sgt.	C
Miller, Henry	Pvt.	E
‡Miller, John	Pvt.	L (KWC)
*Miller, William E.	Pvt.	I
‡Milton, Francis E.	Pvt.	F (KWC)
*Milton, Joseph	Pvt.	F
‡Mitchell, John	Pvt.	I (KWC)
‡Monroe, Joseph	Pvt.	F (KWC)
‡Moody, William	Pvt.	A (KIV)
‡Moonie, George A.	Trmptr.	E (KWC)
‡Moore, Andrew J.	Pvt.	G (KOH)
Moore, Hugh N.	Pvt.	M
Moore, James E.	Farrier	B
Moore, Lansing A.	Pvt.	L
‡Morris, George C.	Cpl.	I (KWC)
†Morris, William E.	Pvt.	M
Morrison, John	Pvt.	G
*Morrow, William E.	Pvt.	B
*Morton, Thomas	Sgt.	D
Moylan, Myles	Capt.	A

*Mueller, William	Pvt.	D
Muering, John	Saddler	A
Mullen, Martin	Pvt.	C
*Muller, John	Pvt.	H
Murphy, Michael	Pvt.	K
*Murphy, Robert L.	Sgt.	I
Murphy, Thomas	Pvt.	K
*Murray, Henry	Cpl.	K
†Murray, Thomas	Sgt.	B
Myers, Frank	Pvt.	F
*Myers, Fred	Pvt.	I
*Nave, Andrew C.	2nd Lt.	I
Nealon, Daniel	Cpl.	H
Neely, Frank	Pvt.	M
Nees, Elder	Pvt.	H
†Newell, Daniel	Blksmth.	M
Nicholas, Joshua S.	Pvt.	H
Nohner, Aloys	Trmptr.	D
*Nolan, John	Cpl.	K
Northeg, Olans H.	Sgt.	G
‡Noshang, Jacob	Pvt.	I (KWC)
Nostrand, Olaf	Pvt.	F
*Nowlan, Henry J.	1st Lt.	QM
Nugent, William D.	Pvt.	A
*Nunan, John	Cpl.	L
‡Nursey, Frederick	Sgt.	F (KWC)
*O'Brien, Thomas	Pvt.	B
‡O'Bryan, John	Pvt.	I (KWC)
‡O'Connell, David J.	Pvt.	L (KWC)
‡O'Conner, Patrick	Pvt.	E (KWC)
‡Ogden, John S.	Sgt.	E (KWC)
‡O'Hara, Miles F.	Sgt.	M (KIV)
O'Mann, William	Pvt.	D
‡Omling, Sebastian	Pvt.	F (KWC)
*O'Neill, Bernard	Pvt.	Band
*O'Neill, James	Pvt.	B
O'Neill, John	Pvt.	B

O'Neill, Thomas	Pvt.	G
*Orr, Charles M.	Pvt.	C
O'Ryan, William	Pvt.	H
Osborne, Augustus	Pvt.	G
O'Toole, Patrick J.	Pvt.	F
Owens, Eugene	Sgt.	I
*Pandtle, Christopher	Pvt.	E
‡Parker, John	Pvt.	I (KWC)
‡Patton, John W.	Trmptr.	I (KWC)
Penwell, George P.	Trmptr.	K
‡Perkins, Charles	Saddler	L (KWC)
Petring, Henry	Pvt.	G
‡Phillips, Edgar	Pvt.	C (KWC)
†Phillips, John	Pvt.	H
Pickard, Edwin H.	Pvt.	F
Pickering, Rufus	Pvt.	F
Pigford, Edward	Pvt.	M
*Pilcher, Albert	Pvt.	F
Pinkston, John S.	Pvt.	H
‡Pitter, Felix J.	Pvt.	I (KWC)
*Pittet, Francis	Pvt.	H
Porter, Henry R.	Ass't. Surg.	HQ
‡**Porter, James E.**	1st Lt.	I (KWC)
*Porter, John	Pvt.	I
‡Post, George	Pvt.	I (KWC)
Powers, Johnny	Pvt.	L
Proctor, George W.	Pvt.	A
Pym, James	Pvt.	B
‡Quinn, James	Pvt.	I (KWC)
*Quinn, John	Pvt.	D
Rafter, John	Sgt.	K
*Ragan, Michael	Pvt.	K
*Ragsdale, John S.	Pvt.	A
*Raichel, Henry W.	Pvt.	K
Ramell, William	Trmptr.	H
Randall, George F.	Pvt.	B

ROSTER

Randall, William J.	Pvt.	F
‡Rapp, John	Pvt.	G (KIV)
‡Rauter, John	Pvt.	C (KWC)
‡Reed, Harry A.	Civ.	(KWC)
Reed, John A.	Pvt.	G
‡Reed, William	Pvt.	I (KWC)
‡Rees, William H.	Pvt.	E (KWC)
Reese, William	Pvt.	E
†Reeves, Francis M.	Pvt.	A
‡Reibold, Christian	Pvt.	L (KWC)
Reid, Elwyn S.	Pvt.	D
*Reilly, Michael	Pvt.	K
‡**Reily, William Van W.**	2nd Lt.	E (w/F, KWC)
Reno, Marcus A.	Major	HQ
‡Reynolds, Charles A.	Civ.	Scout (KIV)
*Ricketts, Joseph	Wagoner	M
†Riley, James T.	Sgt.	E
*Rivers, John	Farrier	I
‡Rix, Edward	Pvt.	C (KWC)
Robb, Eldorado I.	Pvt.	G
Robert, Jonathan	Pvt.	K
‡Roberts, Henry	Pvt.	L (KWC)
Robinson, William	Pvt.	M
‡Rogers, Benjamin F.	Pvt.	G (KIV)
‡Rogers, Walter B.	Pvt.	L (KWC)
‡Rollins, Richard	Pvt.	A (KIV)
‡Rood, Edward	Pvt.	E (KWC)
Rooney, James H.	Pvt.	F
Rose, Peter E.	Sgt.	L
‡Rossbury, John W.	Pvt.	I (KWC)
*Roth, Francis	Pvt.	K
Rott, Louis	Sgt.	K
*Rowland, Robert	Pvt.	G
Roy, Stanislas	Cpl.	A
‡Rudden, Patrick	Pvt.	F (KWC)
*Rudolph, George	Pvt.	Band
‡Russell, James H.	Pvt.	C (KWC)
Russell, Thomas	Sgt.	D
†Rutten, Roman	Pvt.	M

‡Ryan, Daniel	Cpl.	C (KWC)
Ryan, James M.	1st Sgt.	M
Ryan, Stephen L.	Pvt.	B
Ryder, Hobart	Pvt.	M
Rye, William W.	Pvt.	M
*Saas, William	Pvt.	I
*Sadler, William	Pvt.	D
Sager, Hiram W.	Pvt.	B
‡St. John, Ludwick	Pvt.	C (KWC)
Sanders, Charles	Pvt.	D
Sango, Henry	Pvt.	F
‡Saunders, Richard	Pvt.	F (KWC)
Schauer, John	Pvt.	K
‡Schele, Henry	Pvt.	E (KWC)
Schlafer, Christian	Trmptr.	K
*Schleifforth, Paul	Pvt.	F
‡Schmidt, Charles	Pvt.	L (KWC)
Schuetze, Frederick	Pvt.	F
Schwerer, John	Pvt.	K
‡Scollin, Henry M.	Cpl.	M (KIV)
‡Scott, Charles	Pvt.	L (KWC)
Scott, George D.	Pvt.	D
‡Seafferman, Henry	Pvt.	G (KIV)
Seayers, Thomas	Pvt.	A
Seifert, August	Pvt.	K
‡Seiler, John	Cpl.	L (KWC)
‡Selby, Crawford	Saddler	G (KIV)
Senn, Robert	Pvt.	M
Severs, James	Pvt.	M
†Severs, Samuel	Pvt.	H
‡Shade, Samuel S.	Pvt.	C (KWC)
Shaedt, William H.	Pvt.	F
*Shanahan, John	Pvt.	G
‡Sharrow, William H.	Sgt.-Maj.	HQ (KWC)
Shea, Daniel	Pvt.	B
‡Shea, Jeremiah	Pvt.	C (KWC)
Shelton, Charles F.	Pvt.	I
*Sherbon, Thomas	Pvt.	Band

ROSTER

*Sheridan, Michael V.	Capt.	L
‡Short, Nathan[1]	Pvt.	C (KWC)
Siebeleder, Anton	Pvt.	A
‡Siefous, Francis W.	Pvt.	F (KWC)
‡Siemon, Charles	Blksmth.	L (KWC)
‡Siemonson, Bent	Pvt.	L (KWC)
Sievertson, John	Pvt.	M
*Simons, Patrick	Pvt.	B
*Sims, John J.	Pvt.	D
Slaper, William	Pvt.	M
Small, John R.	Pvt.	G
‡Smallwood, William	Pvt.	E (KWC)
‡Smith, Albert A.	Pvt.	E (KWC)
‡**Smith, Algernon E.**	1st Lt.	A (w/E, KWC)
Smith, Charles	Pvt.	I
Smith, Charles H.	Pvt.	I
*Smith, Frederick	Pvt.	K
‡Smith, George E.	Pvt.	M (KIV)
Smith, Henry G.	Pvt.	D
‡Smith, James 1st	Pvt.	E (KWC)
‡Smith, James 2nd	Pvt.	E (KWC)
Smith, John S.	Cpl.	F
Smith, William E.	Pvt.	D
†Smith, William H.	Cpl.	B
Sniffin, Frank	Pvt.	M
‡Snow, Andrew	Pvt.	L (KWC)
Spencer, Abel K.	Pvt.	E
Spinner, Phillip	Pvt.	B
*Sprague, Otto	Pvt.	L
‡Stafford, Benjamin	Pvt.	E (KWC)
‡Stanley, Edward	Pvt.	G (KIV)
‡Staples, Samuel F.	Cpl.	I (KWC)
*Stark, Frank	Pvt.	C
***Stein, C.A.**	Vet.	HQ
Steintker, John R.	Farrier	K
‡Stella, Alexander	Pvt.	E (KWC)
*Stephens, George W.	Pvt.	G
*Sterland, Walter	Pvt.	M
Stevenson, Thomas	Pvt.	G

Stivers, Thomas W.	Pvt.	D
Stoddard, Jacob	Pvt.	L
Stoppel, Henry	Pvt.	C
Stout, Edward	Pvt.	B
Stratton, Frank	Pvt.	M
‡Streing, Frederick	Cpl.	M (KIV)
†Strode, Elijah T.	Pvt.	A
‡Stuart, Alpheus	Pvt.	C (KWC)
‡Stungwitz, Ignatz	Pvt.	C (KWC)
‡**Sturgis, James G.**	2nd Lt.	M (w/E, KWC)
***Sturgis, Samuel D.**	Col.	HQ
*Sullivan, Daniel	Pvt.	G
‡Sullivan, John A.	Pvt.	A (KIV)
Sullivan, Michael M.	Pvt.	E
Sullivan, Timothy	Pvt.	F
Summers, David	Pvt.	M (KIV)
Svengros, Ivan	Pvt.	F
Sventi, William	Pvt.	F
Sweeney, John 1st	Pvt.	C
Sweeney, John 2nd	Pvt.	E
*Sweeney, William	Pvt.	F
‡Sweetzer, Thomas P.	Pvt.	A (KIV)
‡Symms, Darwin L.	Pvt.	I (KWC)
‡Tanner, James T.[2]	Pvt.	M (KOH)
*Taply, David	Pvt.	H
‡Tarbox, Byron	Pvt.	L (KWC)
*Taube, Emil	Pvt.	K
Taylor, Walter O.	Blksmth.	G
Taylor, William O.	Blksmth.	A
‡Teeman, William	Cpl.	F (KWC)
‡Tessier, Edward D.	Pvt.	L (KWC)
‡Thadus, John	Pvt.	C (KWC)
*Thomas, Herbert	Pvt.	I
Thomas, James	Pvt.	B
Thompson, Fred	Pvt.	E
†Thompson, Peter	Pvt.	C
Thornberry, Levy	Pvt.	M
*Thorp, Michael	Pvt.	F
Thorpe, Rollins L.	Pvt.	M

*Tilford, Joseph G.	Major	HQ
*Tinkham, Henry L.	Pvt.	B
Tolan, Frank	Pvt.	D
‡Torrey, William A.	Pvt.	E (KWC)
*Tourtellotte, John E.	Capt.	G
Townsend, Horace	Pvt.	I
*Tritten, John G.	Sgt.	HQ
‡Troy, James E.	Pvt.	I (KWC)
Trumble, William	Pvt.	B
*Tulo, Joseph	Pvt.	G
Tunney, Patrick H.	Pvt.	I
‡Turley, Henry	Pvt.	M (KIV)
‡Tweed, Thomas S.	Pvt.	L (KWC)
*Vahlert, Jacob	Wagoner	C
‡Van Allan, Garret	Pvt.	C (KWC)
*Van Arnim, Julius	Pvt.	C
‡Van Bramer, Charles	Pvt.	I (KWC)
*Van Pelt, William A.	Pvt.	K
‡Van Sant, Cornelius	Pvt.	E (KWC)
‡Varden, Frank E.	1st Sgt.	I (KWC)
†Varner, Thomas B.	Pvt.	M
Varnum, Charles A.	2nd Lt.	A
‡Vetter, Michael	Pvt.	L (KWC)
‡Vickory, John	Sgt.	F (KWC)
*Vinatiori, Felix	Chief	Band
‡Voigt, Henry C.	Pvt.	M (KOH)
†Voit, Otto	Saddler	H
‡Voss, Henry	Chief Trmptr.	HQ (KWC)
†Wagoner, John C.	Civ.	Packer
‡Walker, George	Pvt.	E (KWC)
Walker, Robert	Pvt.	C
Wallace, George D.	1st Lt.	G
Wallace, John W.	Cpl.	G
Wallace, Richard A.	Pvt.	B
‡Walsh, Frederick	Trmptr.	L (KWC)
*Walsh, Michael J.	Pvt.	H
Walsh, Thomas	Pvt.	F

*Walter, Aloyse L.	Pvt.	H
Walther, Amos	Pvt.	L
‡Warner, Oscar L.	Pvt.	C (KWC)
‡Warren, Amos B.	Sgt.	L (KWC)
‡Warren, George A. 1st	Pvt.	F (KWC)
Warren, George A. 2nd	Pvt.	E
Warren, George H.	Pvt.	C
Wasmus, Ernest	Pvt.	K
Watson, James	Pvt.	C
‡Way, Thomas N.	Pvt.	F (KWC)
Weaver, George	Pvt.	M
Weaver, Henry C. (aka "Henry C. Marecz")	Trmptr.	M
Weaver, Howard H.	Pvt.	A
Weeks, James	Pvt.	M
Weir, Thomas B.	Capt.	D
*Weis, John	Pvt.	A
Welch, Charles H.	Pvt.	D
‡Wells, Benjamin	Saddler	G (KIV)
*Wells, John S.	Sgt.	E
West, John	Pvt.	C
Wetzel, Adam	Cpl.	B
‡Whaley, William B.	Pvt.	I (KWC)
Whisten, John	Pvt.	M
†Whitaker, Alfred	Pvt.	C
†White, Charles	Sgt.	M
Whitlow, William	Pvt.	K
*Whytefield, Albert	Wagoner	K
*Widemayer, Ferdinand	Pvt.	M
†Wiedman, Charles W.	Pvt.	M
*Wight, Edwin B.	Pvt.	B
†Wilber, James	Pvt.	M
‡Wild, John	Cpl.	I (KWC)
‡Wilkison, John K.	Sgt.	F (KWC)
Williams, Charles	Pvt.	M
Williams, William C.	Pvt.	H
Williams, William W.	Pvt.	E
*Williamson, Pasavan	Pvt.	G
*Wilson, George A.	Pvt.	K

ROSTER

†Windolph, Charles (aka "Charles Wrangle")	Pvt.	H
‡Winney, De Witt	1st Sgt.	K (KOH)
*Witt, Henry	Pvt.	K
Wood, Fred	Pvt.	L
*Wood, William W.	Farrier	M
*Woodruff, Jerry	Pvt.	E
Woods, Aaron	Pvt.	B
‡Wright, Willis B.	Pvt.	C (KWC)
Wycinski, Steven	Pvt.	E
Wylie, George W.	Cpl.	D
‡Wyman, Henry	Pvt.	C (KWC)
Wynn, James	Pvt.	D
‡**Yates, George W.**	Capt.	F (KWC)
*Zametzer, John	Pvt.	M
Zervanst, Charles	Pvt.	C

OTHER CIVILIAN PACKERS:
William Alexander
Moses E. Flint
John Lamplough
William Lawless
Charles Loeser
Henry McBratney
E.L. Moore

INDIAN SCOUTS:
‡Mitch Bouyer, Crow Intrprtr., KWC
‡Bloody Knife, Arickara, KIV
William Baker, Arickara
‡Bobtailed Bull, Arickara, KIV
William Cross, Arickara
Forked Horn, Arickara
†Goose, Arickara
Robert Jackson, Arickara
William Jackson, Arickara
‡Little Brave, Arickara, KIV
Red Bear, Arickara
Red Foolish Bear, Arickara
Young Hawk, Arickara
Black Fox, Arickara
Bull, Arickara
Charging Bull, Arickara
Pretty Face, Arickara
Red Wolf, Arickara
Soldier, Arickara
Stabbed, Arickara
Strikes the Lodge, Arickara
White Eagle, Arickara
Curly, Crow
Goes Ahead, Crow
Hairy Moccasin, Crow
Half Yellow Face, Crow

Boy Chief, Arickara
Bull in the Water, Arickara
Little Sioux, Arickara
One Feather, Arickara
Red Star, Arickara
Strikes Two, Arickara

White Man Runs Him, Crow
†White Swan, Crow
Bear Waiting, Sioux
Buffalo Ancestor, Sioux
Ca-roo, Sioux
White Cloud, Sioux

RECAPITULATION (June 25-26)

	Present	Absent	Killed	Wounded	Died of Wounds
Officers:	31	17	16	0	0
NCO's:	92	28	45	10	1
Enlisted Men:	513	173	192	38	4
Civilians:	18	0	6	1	0
Indian Scouts:	38	0	4	2	0
TOTALS:	692	218	263	51	5

DISPOSITION OF FATALITIES

	Officers	NCO's	E.M.	Civilians	Indian Scouts	Totals
Killed with Custer:	13	35	158	3	1	210
Killed in the Valley:	3	8	23	2	3	39
Killed on Reno Hill:	0	2	11	1	0	14
TOTALS:	16	45	192	6	4	263

NOTES:

[1] The body of Private Nathan Short of Company C is listed as "killed with Custer," inasmuch as he was a member of the Custer battalion. His body, and the body of his horse, were found in August near the mouth of the Rosebud, south of the Yellowstone River. He apparently escaped from the battlefield. Sgt. Daniel Kanipe of Company C stated that Short was still with the Custer battalion at the time Kanipe was sent with a message for the packtrain commander. How Short died so far from his comrades is one of the mysteries of the Custer Battle.

[2]Private James Tanner was wounded on June 26 and died the following day while still on the field of battle (Reno Hill). He is, therefore, listed here as killed in action.

[3]Corporal George King was the only NCO whose wounds caused his subsequent death. Private David Cooney was promoted to Sergeant on June 28 and died of his wounds on July 20. However, he was not an NCO at the time he was wounded.

[4]Officers include medical staff and veterinarian.

BIBLIOGRAPHY

(This bibliography contains not only the sources cited in this work, but also other books which would be of interest to those seeking additional information on the Battle of the Little Big Horn and its participants.)

Bakeless, John, ed. *The Journals of Lewis and Clark.* New York, 1964
Belle Fourche (SD) *Bee,* (1914)
Bourke, John G. *On the Border With Crook.* Chicago, 1962
Bradley, James H. "Journal of the Sioux Campaign of 1876." *Contributions to the Historical Society of Montana,* Vol. IV, 1896
Brackett, William S. "Custer's Last Battle." *Contributions to the Historical Society of Montana,* Vol. IV, 1903
Brininstool, Earl: *Troopers With Custer.* Harrisburg, 1952
Carroll, John, ed. *The Benteen-Goldin Letters.* New York, 1974
_____. *The Two Battles of the Little Big Horn.* New York, 1974
du Bois, Charles G. *Kick the Dead Lion: A Casebook of the Custer Battle.* Billings, MT, 1961
Edgerly, Winfield S. "Narrative," ed. by Charles G. du Bois. Rapid City, SD, *Journal,* 1967
Ellison, Douglas W. *Sole Survivor.* Aberdeen, 1983
Frost, Lawrence A. *The Custer Album.* New York, 1954
_____. *Custer Legends.* Bowling Green, OH, 1981
Graham, W.A. *The Custer Myth.* New York, 1953
Green, Jerome. *Evidence and the Custer Enigma.* Reno, 1979
Grinnell, George B. *The Cheyenne Indians.* Norman, 1963
_____. *The Fighting Cheyennes.* Norman, 1983
Hammer, Kenneth. *Custer in '76.* Provo, 1976

Hardorff, Richard G. *Shadows Along the Little Big Horn.* Seattle, 1977
———. *Markers, Artifacts and Indian Testimony.* Short Hills, NJ, 1985
Hart, B.H. Liddell. *Strategy.* New York, 1974
Horn, W. Don. *Witnesses for the Defense.* Short Hills, NJ, 1981
Hyde, George E. *Spotted Tail's Folks.* Norman, 1961
Kavanagh, Martin. *La Verendrye, His Life and Times.* Norwich, Eng., 1968
Kuhlman, Charles. *Legend Into History.* Harrisburg, 1951
Libby, O.G., ed. *The Arickara Narrative.* New York, 1973
Linderman, Frank B. *Plenty Coups, Chief of the Crows.* Lincoln, 1962
Luce, Edward S. *Keogh, Comanche, and Custer.* St. Louis, 1939
Marquis, Thomas B. *Wooden Leg: A Warrior Who Fought Custer.* Lincoln, 1931
———. *Custer On the Little Bighorn.* Lodi, 1967
Miles, Nelson A. *Personal Recollections.* Chicago, 1896
Monaghan, Jay. *Custer.* Lincoln, 1959
Nelson, Bruce. *Land of the Dacotahs.* Minneapolis, 1946
Schell, Herbert S. *History of South Dakota.* Lincoln, 1968
South Dakota Codified Laws, Vol. I, "Indian Treaties."
Stands In Timber, John. *Cheyenne Memories.* New Haven, 1967
Stewart, Edgar I. *Custer's Luck.* Norman, 1955
Upton, Richard, ed. *The Custer Adventure.* Crow Agency (MT), 1981
Utley, Robert M. *Custer Battlefield.* Washington, DC, 1969
Vaughn, J.W. *Indian Fights.* Norman, 1966
Washburn, Wilcomb E., ed. *The American Indian and the United States.* New York, 1973

NOTES

CHAPTER ONE

[1] *Land of the Dacotahs,* by Bruce Nelson. (Minneapolis, 1946) p. 10.

[2] *La Verendrye, His Life and Times.* by Martin Kavanagh. (Norwich, Eng., 1968) In 1732, the Sioux were living near Red Lake, Minnesota, extending from there to Lake of the Woods. (p. 97)

A map of La Verendrye's travels (and those of his sons) from 1731 to 1753, shows the "Horse Indians" (Cheyennes) occupying the Black Hills and most of South Dakota west of the Missouri River. The Sioux were on the Missouri's east bank at present-day Pierre, and on the west bank at the confluence of White River. The Arickaras lived north of Pierre along the east bank, and a band of Poncas occupied the west bank. (Map opp. p. 208)

[3] The first village of Sioux was found at the mouth of the James River on the east side of the Missouri, and the second village was at the mouth of the Bad River (present-day Ft. Pierre) on the west bank. Captain Clark described the first group as "a small village." "The Journals of Lewis and Clark," edited by John Bakeless (Mentor, 1964).

The Ogallala and Brule Sioux reached the James River valley in eastern South Dakota about 1760. Fifteen years later (1775) the Ogallalas crossed the Missouri below the Great Bend, then spread to Bad River where Lewis and Clark found them in 1804. *History of South Dakota,* by Herbert S. Schell. (Lincoln, 1968), pp. 20 and 41.

[4] *The Cheyenne Indians,* by George Bird Grinnell. (Norman, 1963), pp. 36-37.

[5] *Ibid.,* p. 37; *History of South Dakota, op. cit.,* p. 20.

[6] *Ibid.* pp. 36-37

[7] *Wooden Leg: A Warrior Who Fought Custer,* interpreted by Thomas B. Marquis. (Lincoln, 1931 reprint), p. 1.

[8] *The Cheyenne Indians, op. cit.,* p. 35.

[9] *Plenty Coups, Chief of the Crows,* by Frank B. Linderman. (Lincoln, 1962)

[10] *Spotted Tail's Folks,* by George E. Hyde. (Norman, 1961)

[11] *The American Indian and the United States,* A Documentary History, Vol. IV, compiled by Wilcomb E. Washburn, Smithsonian Institution. (New York, 1973), p. 2477.

[12] *Ibid.,* p. 2478.

[13] *Cheyenne Memories,* by John Stands-In-Timber. (New Haven, 1967), p. 162.

[14] *Ibid.,* p. 54.

[15] Annual Report of Brigadier General George Crook, 23 Sept. 1876.

[16] *The American Indian and the United States, op. cit.,* pp. 2518-19.

[17] South Dakota Codified Laws, Vol. 1, Art. 1, Document 20: "Indian Treaties," p. 117.

[18] Annual Report to the Commissioner of Indian Affairs, Sept. 10, 1875.

[19] *On the Border With Crook,* by John G. Bourke. (Chicago, 1962)

[20] The itinerary of the hostiles which follows is a summary of pages 169-92 of *Wooden Leg, op. cit.*

[21] *Wooden Leg,* p. 186 note.

CHAPTER TWO

[1] *Indian Fights,* by J.W. Vaughn. (Norman, 1966), pp. 122-26.

[2] *Ibid.,* pp. 119-20.

[3] *Ibid.,* pp. 126-28.

[4] *Wooden Leg, op. cit.,* pp. 193-97.

[5] *Ibid.,* p. 204.

[6] *Ibid.,* pp. 197-99.

[7] *Indian Fights, op. cit.,* pp. 128-29.

[8] *Ibid.,* pp. 129-38.

[9] *The Fighting Cheyennes,* by George Bird Grinnell. (Norman, 1915, 7th printing, 1983), p. 336; *Cheyenne Memories,* by John Stands-In-Timber, *op. cit.,* pp. 188-89.

NOTES

CHAPTER THREE

[1] Bradley, Lt. James H: "Journal of the Sioux Campaign of 1876." *Contributions to the Historical Society of Montana*, Vol. IV, 1896, p. 216.

[2] "General Godfrey's Narrative," reprinted in *The Custer Myth*, by Col. W.A. Graham. (New York, 1953), p. 134. (Hereinafter referred to as "Godfrey Narrative").

[3] Carroll, John. *Benteen-Goldin Letters*. (New York, 1974), p. 162.

[4] "The Edgerly Narrative," by General Winfield S. Edgerly. This narrative is the text of a lecture which Edgerly delivered in several cities in 1898. It was first published by Charles G. du Bois in the Rapid City (SD) *Journal*, on June 25-27, 1967.

[5] *Ibid.*

[6] Godfrey Narrative, p. 134.

[7] Carroll, *Benteen-Goldin Letters*, pp. 164-65.

[8] *The Two Battles of the Little Big Horn*, edited by John M. Carroll. (New York, 1974). General Brisbin's letter to General Godfrey is reprinted here in full.

[9] *The Custer Myth, op. cit.*, pp. 261-62. In an interview with Walter Camp in 1909, Herendeen said, "Early on June 25 I told Custer that Tullock's Creek was just over the divide, but Custer replied rather impatiently to the effect that there was now no occasion for sending me there as the Indians were known to be in his front, and that his command had been discovered by them. He said the only thing for him [Custer] to do was therefore to charge their village as soon as possible." Hammer, Kenneth. *Custer in '76*. (Provo, 1976), p. 221.

[10] Edgerly Narrative.

[11] Godfrey Narrative, p. 136.

[12] *The Custer Myth*, p. 216.

[13] Godfrey Narrative, p. 148; see also *Custer Legends*, by Dr. Lawrence A. Frost. (Bowling Green, 1981), pp. 197-98.

[14] Godfrey Narrative, p. 130.

[15] *Ibid.*, p. 148.

[16] This information on the actual course of the Rosebud could only have been given to Terry by Mitch Bouyer and the other Crow scouts who knew this area thoroughly. The official map used at the conference aboard the *Far West* shows the upper reaches of the streams in this area (including the Rosebud) by dotted lines which are far from accurate. General Sheridan described the area as "an almost totally unknown region, comprising an area of 90,000 square miles." ("Custer's Last Battle," by William S. Brackett, reprinted in *Contributions to the Historical Society of Montana*, Vol. IV [1903], p. 259.)

[17] Edgerly Narrative.

[18] Wallace, Official Report. Edgerly made the same statement in his narrative. See also: Godfrey Narrative, p. 138.

[19] Edgerly Narrative.

[20] *Ibid.*

CHAPTER FOUR

[1] Wooden Leg, p. 203

[2] *Ibid.*, pp. 203-205.

[3] *Ibid.*, p. 206; *Custer's Luck*, by Edgar I. Stewart. (Norman, 1955), pp. 309-12. Dr. Stewart, after reviewing the estimates of participants, both military and Indian (as well as those "authorities" not present), concluded that there were not more than 4000 warriors, and possibly not that many, a conclusion in which the present writer concurs.

[4] Wooden Leg, p. 216.

[5] See: Roster, Appendix

[6] Carroll, *Benteen-Goldin Letters*, p. 147.

[7] *Ibid.*, p. 154.

[8] Edgerly Narrative.

[9] Gibson, Lt. Francis; Letter to George L. Yates, son of Bvt. Lt. Col. George W. Yates, captain of "F" Co., dated April 28, 1915. This letter is now in the Custer Battlefield Museum collection.

[10] Ellison, Douglas, *Sole Survivor*, Appendix III, p. 111.

[11] *Ibid.*, p. 96ff. The four men who dropped out of the Custer Battalion, apparently before Custer reached Cedar Coulee, were Farrier John

Fitzgerald, Privates James Watson, Peter Thompson and John Brennan, all of Company "C." All rejoined the Reno-Benteen forces on Reno Hill. Pvt. Dennis Lynch of Company "F" who was with the packtrain told Walter Camp that Frank Hunter, a private in Co. "F," was on duty with his company as part of the Custer battalion. He claimed that Hunter's horse ran away with him, crossing the Little Big Horn at the mouth of Medicine Tail Coulee, then carried him through the Uncpapa camp over to Reno's battleground where he was able to ascend the bluffs and join Reno's command on the hill. Although Hunter is listed as a survivor of the battle, Lynch's story (probably told him by Hunter) is too incredible to be taken seriously, for this would make Hunter a witness to Custer's final battle, and historians would never have overlooked him!

One man, Frank Finkel, later claimed to be a survivor of the Custer Battle, and his story has been told by Dr. Charles Kuhlman in a manuscript published in 1972 (*Massacre Survivor!"* [Old Army Press, Fort Collins]) and by Douglas Ellison (*Sole Survivor*, [Aberdeen, 1983]). Quite apart from the interesting story of Finkel, Ellison's book, in Appendix III, has provided students of the Custer battle with the most complete and informative statistics available. The Roster in the Appendix of this present work, although prepared by the author in the mid-'60's, has been checked against Ellison's tables and is in complete agreement with them.

[12] Kuhlman, Charles, *Legend Into History*. (Harrisburg, 1951); Dr. Kuhlman's phrase, the title of his chapter 4, has been borrowed by the present writer for this chapter.

[13] *Ibid.*, p. 87 and note 35.

[14] Graham, *The Custer Myth*, pp. 142, 203.

[15] The exact wording of this order is not known. Col. Reno, in his Official Report, said he was told "to move forward at as rapid a gait as he thought prudent, and to charge afterwards and that the whole outfit would support."

[16] Letter to the author from Major Edward S. Luce, former Superintendent of the Custer Battlefield, and a former member of the 7th Cavalry, dated February 26, 1953.

There is, however, another gait called a "canter" or "lope," which resembles an easy gallop — faster than a trot, but slower than a gallop, which would cover about 1 mile every 6 minutes. It should also be noted that a horse, when climbing a hill or slope, will always go as fast as the angle of ascent will allow, usually at a canter or a gallop.

[17] Hammer, *Custer in '76*, pp. 231-32.

[18] An interesting alternative (or addition) to this theory is provided by the interview of Sergeant Daniel Kanipe by Walter Camp in 1908. Kanipe stated that he saw a number of Indians (60 or 75 of them) on the bluffs just north of Reno hill, and that he reported this to his 1st Sergeant, Edwin Bobo, who passed the information on to Custer through the company officers. General Custer immediately turned to the right in the direction of the Indians. Kanipe told Camp that he believed this was what determined Custer to cease following Reno and to turn north, presumably to drive these Indians back to the village. (Hammer, *op. cit.* pp. 92-97). Whether it was this sighting or Cooke's report (or both) that caused Custer to swing to the north at this point cannot be known. However the presence of this band of Indians is no surprise; the Indians Gerard had spotted from the Lone Tepee never did reach the village until after the battle, which means they must have turned off before reaching the river, where they must have turned north.

[19] *Ibid.*, pp. 93-94.

[20] Graham, *The Custer Myth*, p. 290.

[21] Hardorff, Richard, "Shadows Along the Little Big Horn," the *Garry Owen 1976 Annual of the Little Big Horn Associates*, (Seattle, 1977), p. 113.

[22] The testimony regarding this incident is so contradictory that a resolution of it is probably impossible. Part of the problem may be attributed to the fact that Private Martin spoke little English and Curly spoke none. We must depend, so far as Curly's testimony is concerned, on the ability of the interpreter to understand both the Crow language and the English in such a way as to enable him to communicate Curly's account faithfully —assuming that Curly himself was telling the truth. With both Martin and Curly there remains the unfortunate toll taken upon human memory by advanced age, and many of their accounts were given in their twilight years. As for Lieutenant DeRudio, his reputation for veracity was not highly regarded, at least by Benteen, and later by General Hugh Scott. Whether DeRudio's critics were justified will never be known.

[23] Graham, *The Custer Myth*, p. 290.

[24] Stewart, *Custer's Luck*, p. 317, and note 33.

[25] Kuhlman, *Legend Into History*, p. 223, note 35.

[26] Edgerly Narrative.

[27] Graham, *The Custer Myth*, p. 180; in his statement to the *New York Herald*,

NOTES

Aug. 8, 1876, Benteen said, "The whole time occupied in this march was about an hour and a half." (*Custer Myth*, p. 227), which added to 12:10 p.m. would be 1:40 p.m.

[28] Kuhlman, *op.cit.*, p. 223, note 35.

[29] Godfrey, in his narrative, said 12-15 miles; Benteen, in his Feb. 2, 1892, letter to Goldin, said 15 miles; in the Feb. 10, 1896, letter, "15 or more miles," and in the Mar. 14, 1896, letter, "10-12 miles;" Edgerly, in his Reno Court testimony, said 14 miles.

[30] Graham, *The Custer Myth*, pp. 138, 180.

[31] Hammer, *Custer in '76*, interview with Godfrey, p. 75. One officer was heard to ask, "I wonder what the old man [Benteen] is keeping us here so long for?"

[32] *Ibid.*, p. 93, note 11.

CHAPTER FIVE

[1] Hammer, *Custer in '76* p. 112.

[2] *Ibid.*, p. 106.

[3] *Ibid.*, p. 133.

[4] Testifying at the Reno Court of Inquiry, DeRudio said that he saw Custer, Cooke, and one other man on the highest point on the right bank of the river, just below where Dr. DeWolf was killed. He said it was not Weir Point, but one nearer the river, where the Little Big Horn comes right under the bluffs, and that Custer waved his hat and disappeared. He estimated it was six or seven minutes after the troops reached the timber, and five or six minutes before the retreat began. (Official Transcript, 491-93, 498-505).

[5] Hammer, *op. cit.*, p. 118.

[6] Ellison, *Sole Survivor*, p. 41; Private William Morris, however, told Camp that Smith was killed at the edge of the timber. (Hammer, p. 131).

[7] Hammer, p. 143.

[8] DeRudio told Walter Camp that he picked up the wounded Sergeant White's gun on the skirmish line, and as White was subsequently in the timber, we can only assume that DeRudio helped him reach it. (Hammer, pp. 84, 141).

[9] Hammer, pp. 118, 143, 148.

[10] *Wooden Leg*, p. 217.

[11] *Ibid.*, p. 219.

[12] *Ibid.*, p. 217.

[13] Edgerly narrative.

[14] Reno Court.

[15] *Ibid.;* Lt. Varnum said: "I don't know whether there were any Indians in the timber before the command left or not. I didn't see any myself. When we first got a chance to talk about it, after we got on the hill, I heard there were Indians behind us in the woods. Some of the men were making such a remark. When I went to get the horses I had no trouble getting them. There were no Indians in where the animals were. Some of the men who had been left as horse-holders were probably firing. The line on the left of the timber was under the same hill that the horses were. All I had to do was to ride down the skirmish line, to and beyond the left of the line. Captain Moylan said the Indians were getting in on his left, and that the horses were not covered by the skirmish line, and that the Indians would probably get in there. I didn't see any Indians in there; neither did I find or see any horses that had been struck by bullets." (*Troopers With Custer*, by Earl Brininstool, Harrisburg, 1952), p. 112.

[16] Reno Court.

[17] Hammer, p. 112.

[18] *Ibid.*, p. 112.

[19] *Ibid.*, p. 118.

[20] *Wooden Leg*, pp. 220-21.

[21] Hammer, p. 119.

[22] *Ibid.*, p. 133.

[23] *Ibid.*, p. 107.

[24] *Wooden Leg*, p. 223.

[25] Hammer, p. 119.

[26] *Ibid.*, p. 133.

[27] Grinnell, *The Fighting Cheyennes*, p. 349.

NOTES

CHAPTER SIX

[1] Graham, *Custer Myth*, p. 142.

[2] Hammer, p. 85; Lt. DeRudio told Walter Camp that as he moved back into the timber after the command retreated, the Indians ceased firing and set up what DeRudio called "a peculiar cry." "Wondering what this could mean," said Camp, "DeRudio looked out and saw the Indians pointing to the bluffs and Benteen's battalion was in full view. DeRudio says this is what saved Reno's battalion from entire destruction. The appearance of Benteen checked the pursuit after Reno." This is probably correct, but it was the subsequent sighting of Custer's battalion further north that caused the main body of Indians who had defeated Reno to ride off toward the upper camps.

[6] Hammer, p. 66. McDougall said that Hare met them a half-mile east of Reno Hill, but Hare said the round trip took him 20 minutes, so the packtrain must have been further away than a half-mile, and insisted that it was "a mile or not much more from Reno."

[4] Edgerly Narrative.

[5] Hammer, p. 66.

[6] *Ibid.*, p. 66, 69.

[7] *Ibid.*, p. 70.

[8] Graham, *The Custer Myth*, p. 142.

[9] Hammer, p. 70.

[10] According to Major E.S. Luce, onetime member of the 7th Cavalry, the order to Benteen remained his, and could only be rescinded by Custer himself. Major General Duane L. Corning, retired Adjutant General of South Dakota, concurs.

[11] Official Transcript, 1002; 821.

[12] Hammer, p. 70.

[13] *Ibid.*, p. 62.

[14] Edgerly Narrative.

[15] Brininstool, *Capt. Benteen's Story*, p. 23.

[16] Hammer, pp. 70-71.

[17] Edgerly Narrative.

[18] Hammer, pp. 66-67.

19. *Ibid.*, p. 81.
20. *Ibid.*, p. 67.
21. Graham, *Custer Myth*, p. 228.
22. *Ibid.*, p. 228.
23. Edgerly Narrative.
24. Hammer, p. 57.
25. Graham, *The Custer Myth*, p. 143.
26. *Ibid.*, p. 143.
27. Hammer, pp. 57, 67, 113, 241.
28. Graham, *The Custer Myth*, p. 244.
29. Edgerly Narrative.
30. Hammer, p. 81.
31. *Ibid.*, p. 33; *see also:* Stewart, *Custer's Luck*, p. 421.
32. Hammer, p. 120.
33. *Ibid.*, p. 120, note 5.
34. *Ibid.*, p. 120, note 5.
35. *Ibid.*, p. 114.
36. Edgerly Narrative.
37. Hammer, p. 134 and 152.
38. *Ibid.*, p. 114.
39. *Ibid.*, pp. 114-15. Pvt. John Foley adds himself, and Sergeants John Rafter and Louis Rott, all of "K" Company, p. 147.

   The list of Medal of Honor recipients excludes some of those already mentioned and adds the names of others. *See:* Hammer, p. 268.
40. *Ibid.*, pp. 114-15.
41. Graham, *The Custer Myth*, p. 245. Peter Thompson of Company "C," whose horse had given out while riding with the Custer command, and had taken refuge with Reno's forces on the hill, told his story of the battle in 1914 to the Belle Fourche (SD) *Bee.* He said that when he "came to where the horses were huddled together, I heard a voice feebly calling my name. Looking up the direction of the sound I saw a man by the name of Tanner lying close to some sage brush. Some one had thrown the cape of an overcoat

over him to protect him from the sun. Kneeling down by his side I asked him what I could do for him. He told me he was done for and asked me to get him a drink of water. I saw from the nature of his wound that his hours were numbered. I secured a blanket on which I placed him. Having only one hand with which to do the work" (earlier that day he had been shot through the right arm and hand) "I found it hard to move him. I then got an overcoat and made a pillow for his head and used my overcoat to shelter him." Thompson then found some empty canteens and made another trip down the ravine to the river. When he returned, he went to see "how Tanner was getting along. When I approached the place where I had left him I saw a man tugging away at the overcoat which I had placed under his head. Rushing forward I seized the man by the coat collar and sent him sprawling on the ground some distance away... After he had gone I turned to Tanner and found that he was dead. He had died before his wish for a drink of water could be gratified." This account would seem to support Sergeant Ryan's story that Tanner died shortly after he was wounded, later in the day, June 26.

The author is indebted to Mr. Marion Lucca, Editor of the Belle Fourche *Daily Post* and *Weekly Bee*, for providing him with a copy of Thompson's story entitled, "The Experience of a Private Soldier In the Custer Massacre."

[42] Hammer, pp. 115 and 120.

CHAPTER SEVEN

[1] Reno's Report. "I deployed, and with the Ree scouts on my left, charged down the valley, driving the Indians with great ease for about 2½ miles. I, however, soon saw that I was being drawn into some trap, as they certainly would fight harder."

[2] B.H. Liddell Hart, *Strategy*, Signet reprint, (New York, 1974).

[3] Hammer, p. 103, note 2. "Martin says he was with Custer after he passed the high ground and left him just as the command started down a ravine to get off the bluff, somewhat to the right of highest ground [Weir Point] and about 1000 feet from it."

[4] *Ibid.*, p. 166. In answer to Camp's question, "Did you see Reno retreat?" Curly said, "Yes, saw retreat and Bouyer then gave signal to Custer. Custer and Tom Custer returned signal by waving hats, and men cheered." Obviously Curly did not understand the question, for it is ridiculous to believe that Reno's retreat would be applauded with cheers.

⁵*Ibid.*, p. 172.

⁶Letter of Walter Camp to Charles Woodruff, Feb. 28, 1910; Walter Camp Collection, box 9, folder 11, BYU Library.

⁷*Wooden Leg*, pp. 224-29.

⁸This action could have served a double purpose. Custer could also have been trying to signal Benteen of his whereabouts.

⁹In his last account, given to General Hugh Scott and translated by Russell White Bear, Curly said that "one of the troops (this troop had gray horses)... turned its direction toward the Little Horn. Custer with the remainder of his command *continued going northward* — his trail was about 1½ miles from the river." It was at this point that Curly was dismissed. Graham, *Custer Myth*, p. 18.

¹⁰*Benteen-Goldin Letters*, Carroll; (New York, 1974), pp. 155 and 158.

¹¹Hammer, pp. 212-13. The "flat near the ford" is some distance from the river, just below the "first rise (where Foley lay)." This is approximately the point referred to by Benteen as being "six furlongs" (660 yards) from the river.

¹²*Ibid.*, pp. 206-7.

¹³*Ibid.*, p. 116.

¹⁴*Ibid.*, pp. 214-15.

¹⁵Graham, *Custer Myth*, p. 90.

¹⁶*Ibid.*, Godfrey Narrative, p. 94.

¹⁷Jerome Greene, *Evidence and the Custer Enigma*, (Reno, 1979 reprint).

¹⁸In the early 1950's, Major Luce, then Superintendent of the Custer Battlefield National Monument, told the author that one of his predecessors had gathered up a large number of expended cartridge cases from the firing range at old Fort Custer, a few miles north of the Battlefield, and spread them around the Custer Battlefield so that visitors would be able to find "souvenirs" to take with them. We raised this point at the Little Big Horn Associates meeting in Bismarck, North Dakota, in July, 1985, when a panel of archeologists reported on their work at the Battlefield. We were told that in 1877, when Fort Custer was built, all new cartridges made for the army were stamped with the year of manufacture, and that this would disqualify any remaining casings from Fort Custer as being authentic relics of the

battle. On returning home from that meeting, the author examined his collection of casings which he had found at Fort Custer and found no date on any of them, which suggests that the ammunition used on the firing range at Fort Custer was old issue, a situation that eventually would change after all the pre-1877 ammunition had been used up. This fact does cast some doubt on the authenticity of some of the casings found on the Battlefield in recent times.

[19] Hardorff, *Markers*, p. 29, citing Camp Mss. 559. However, Lt. DeRudio said that the first dead man was found about 150 yards from the river.

[20] Edgar I. Stewart, *Custer's Luck*, p. 466, said that "A number of beheaded white bodies so mutilated as to be unrecognizable were also found," citing General Godfrey in his "Address on the Fortieth Anniversary of the Custer Battle." Richard G. Hardorff, *Markers, Artifacts and Indian Testimony*, p. 27, cites a 1907 interview of the Cheyenne, Two Moons, by a Mr. Throssel, in which the Cheyenne warrior said that some of the soldier bodies were "afterward dragged into the village, dismembered and burned at big dance that night." Citing an article in the Hardin (MT) *Tribune*, June 22, 1923, Stewart says "there were the heads of three men fastened together with wires and suspended from a lodgepole. The hair had all been burned off, and the heads could not be identified." (*Custer's Luck*, p. 466). Private John Foley of Company "K," (not to be confused with the Corporal John Foley mentioned elsewhere), said in a Camp interview that he found the head of a corporal of G troop under an overturned kettle. This corporal had red hair. (Hammer, p. 147). Mr. Camp in a footnote named James Martin and Otto Hagemann as corporals of G Company who were killed in the Reno fight, but said that both of them had brown hair. It is possible that dried blood in the hair of the unfortunate whose head Foley found simply gave the impression that the man had red hair. Foolish Elk, an Ogallala warrior, said that no soldiers, dead or alive, were taken into the village, and Turtle Rib, a Minneconjou Sioux, said only that they took no soldiers off the battlefield alive. (Hammer, pp. 199 and 202.)

[21] *Wooden Leg*, p. 239.

[22] Grinnell, *The Fighting Cheyennes*, pp. 350-51.

[23] *Ibid.*, p. 350.

[24] Hammer, p. 207.

[25] Hammer, pp. 224 and 234. Herendeen said, "About ½ hour after the troops

had retreated from the timber, firing began down the river. This firing... consisted of a great many volleys, with scattering shots between the volleys."

[26] *Wooden Leg*, p. 230.

[27] *Ibid.*, p. 231.

[28] *Ibid.*, p. 231.

[29] Thomas B. Marquis, *Custer On the Little Bighorn*, (Lodi, Cal., 1967), p. 38.

[30] David F. Barry, *Indian Notes on the Custer Battle*, edited by Usher L. Burdick, (Baltimore, 1937), pp. 25-27.

[31] "Edgerly says one of E Troop's gray horses was found wounded at the river near Custer battlefield, and appeared to be much frightened and very shy but followed the troops at a distance all way to crossing of the Yellowstone." (Hammer, p. 58). It is not known what happened to this horse, but perhaps Gibbon's men took it with them. There are other stories of horses found alive but badly wounded, and they were presumably shot.

[32] *Wooden Leg*, p. 232

[33] Marquis, *Custer On the Little Bighorn*, p. 39.

[34] *Wooden Leg*, pp. 232-33.

[35] Hammer, p. 207.

[36] *Wooden Leg*, p. 230.

[37] Hammer, p. 87.

[38] *Ibid.*, p. 213.

[39] *Ibid.*, pp. 116-17. Jerome Greene (*Evidence and the Custer Enigma*, p. 39) says that "In 1904, Joseph Blummer picked up a boot containing human bones in the same area [Deep Coulee]. Initialed 'J.D.,' it probably bespoke the fate of Trooper John Duggan of Company L." It might also have been the boot of Private John Darris of "E" Company.

[40] *Ibid.*, p. 134.

[41] *Ibid.*, pp. 79, 136, 139.

[42] *Ibid.*, p. 248.

[43] *Ibid.*, pp. 72, 79, 136, 147.

[44] Graham, *Custer Myth*, p. 18.

[45] Hammer, p. 149.
[46] Ellison, *Sole Survivor*, pp. 54-55.
[47] Graham, *Custer Myth*, p. 146.
[48] Hammer, p. 48.
[49] *Ibid.*, p. 251.
[50] *Ibid.*, p. 137.
[51] *Ibid.*, p. 51.
[52] *Ibid.*, p. 137.
[53] *Ibid.*, p. 146.
[54] *Ibid.*, p. 248.
[55] *Ibid.*, p. 120.
[56] *Ibid.*, p. 126.
[57] *Ibid.*, p. 226. "Henley" apparently refers to Sergeant Hanley, for no Henley was present with the regiment at the Little Big Horn. (*See:* Note 45.)
[58] *Wooden Leg*, pp. 236-37.

NOTES: EPILOGUE

[1] "Up to the moment of Custer's attack no information was had, public or private, to justify the belief that there were in Sitting bull's camp more than 500 or 800 warriors." (Brackett, p. 260.)
[2] Edgerly Narrative.
[3] Graham, *Custer Myth*, p. 134.
[4] *Ibid.*, p. 194.
[5] *Ibid.*, p. 312.
[6] *Ibid.*, p. 141.
[7] *Ibid.*, p. 147.
[8] Edgerly Narrative.
[9] Hammer, p. 233.
[10] Miles, Gen. Nelson A., *Personal Recollections*, (Chicago, 1896), p. 290.

INDEX

Adams, Pvt. Jacob: 124, 127
Agreement of 1876: 25
Apache Indians: 25
Arapahoe Indians: 21
Arickara Indian scouts: 22, 30, 59, 62, 171
Assiniboine Indians: 22, 31

Bad River of South Dakota: 171
Bancroft, Pvt. Neil: 93
Barry, David F: 118
Belle Fourche (SD) *Bee:* 181
Benteen, Col. F.W: 63, 94, 107, 112, 115-16, 118, 122-23, 131, 176, 179, 181-82, march up the Rosebud, 44-46; assigned battalion, 57; on reconnaissance to left, 57-58, 66-67, 176-77; battalion statistics, 60; at the morass, 68, 177; receives order: "Come on, Be quick." 69; joins Reno battalion on the bluffs, 81-82; moves to Weir Point, 84-86; returns to Reno Hill, 88; during hilltop defense, June 26, 91-92; comments on Custer at Medicine Tail Ford, 109; opinion of Reno's position in the timber, 133; criticism of Custer's strategy, 131-32; his actions reviewed, 134-35; seen approaching Reno Hill, 179
"Big Bend" of the Rosebud: 36-37, 129
Bighead, Kate: 116, 120
Big Horn Mountains: 50, 95
Big Horn River: 43, 48, 50, 55, 126
Bismarck (ND) *Tribune:* 60
Blackfeet Sioux Indians: 31
Black Hills Expedition of 1874: 24

Black Hills of South Dakota: 22-23, 171
Bloody Knife, Arickara scout: 59, 76
Blummer, Joseph: 107, 184
Bobo, 1st Sgt. Edwin: 119, 176
Boren, Pvt. Ansgarius: 93
Bourke, Lt. John G: 28-29
Bouyer, Michel "Mitch": 174, 181, on scouting Tulloch's Creek, 46-47; assigned to Custer's battalions, 60; views Reno fight from Weir Point, 66-67, 100-01; reports back to Custer in Medicine Tail, 102, 104
Bozeman, Montana: 27
Bozeman Trail: 24
Bradley, Lt. James: 42
Brennan, Pvt. John: 175
Brisbin, Major James: 46
Brule Sioux Indians: 22, 31, 171
Buffalo Calf Road Woman, Cheyenne: 39
Bureau of Indian Affairs: 26, 45, 130
Burkman, Pvt. John: 59, 67
Busby, Montana: 49
Bustard, Sgt. James: 119
Butler, 1st Sgt. James: 110

Calhoun, Lt. James: 56, 59, 103, 119, 121
Calhoun Ridge: 110, 117-18, 121, reached by Yates' battalion, 115; Keogh battalion joins Yates there, 116; troops there attacked, 119
Callahan, Cpl. John: 59
Camp Marker: 67
Camp Walter: 65-66, 94, 101-02, 108-11, 123-27, 131, 133, 175-77, 179, 181, 183
Cartwright, R.G: 107

Cedar Coulee: 66, 107, 174, reached by Custer, 65, 100, 103; reached by Edgerly, 85; reached by Boston Custer, 115
Chalk Butte, Montana: 31
Chambers, Major Alex: 34
Charley, Pvt. Vincent: 88
Cheyenne Indians: 25-26, 29, 33, 63, 109, 129, migrate from Missouri River to Black Hills, 21; lose Black Hills to Sioux by treaty, 23; attacked by Reynolds on Powder River, 27-28; join Ogallalas, Uncpapas and Minneconjous, 30; joined by other Sioux tribes and other Cheyenne bands, 31; camp sites on Rosebud River, 32; scouts observe soldiers south of Rosebud, 34; scouts report back to chiefs, 36; join Sioux in Battle of the Rosebud, 39; move from Reno Creek to Little Big Horn, 55-56; Little Wolf's band seen by Gerard, 61; appraisal of Reno's retreat, 80; long distance firing at Custer, 107; with Ogallalas in Deep Ravine, 116; lead assault on Sturgis' platoon, 117-18; occupy Black Hills, 171
Cheyenne Reservation, Montana: 49
Cheyenne River of South Dakota: 21
Chippewa (Ojibway) Indians: 20
Clapp, Dexter E: 26
Clark, Capt. William: 171
Clear Creek, Wyoming: 33
Coleman, Pvt. Thomas W: 93
Colstrip, Montana: 32
Comanche Indians: 21
"Comanche," Keogh's horse: 119
Comes In Sight, Cheyenne warrior: 39
Congress, U.S: 22
Cooke, Lt. Col. William W: 59, 98, 176, receives Gerard's report, 64; gives Martin message for Benteen, 65, 100; body found near Custer, 122; seen on the bluffs by DeRudio, 177
Corning, Maj. Gen. Duane L: 179
Crazy Horse, Ogallala warrior: 28, 30, 118
Crazy Horse "Canyon" (ravine): 118, 121
Crittenden, Lt. John J: 59, 119
Crook, Gen. George: 26, 45, 50, 56, 61, 126, fight on Powder River, 27-28; Battle of the Rosebud, 37-40; appraisal of his part in the campaign, 129-30
Crow Agency, Montana: 29
Crowley, Pvt. Cornelius: 93
Crow King, Uncpapa warrior: 118
Crow Reservation, Montana: 24, 26
Crow Indians: 21-24
Crow Scouts: 174, join Gibbon's command at Crow Agency, 29; others join Crook's command on Goose Creek, 33; at the Battle of the Rosebud, 37; discover hostiles' trail leaving Rosebud, 49; accompany Reno battalion, 59; dismissed by Bouyer, 100, 104
Curly, Crow scout: 65, 127, went with Bouyer to Weir Point, 66, 100; met Custer in Medicine Tail Coulee, 66, 104; claimed to have seen Reno retreat, 101, 181; reliability as a witness, 108, 176; saw Custer send another messenger from Medicine Tail Coulee, 123; saw Custer turn north from Medicine Tail, 182
Custer Battlefield, Montana: 107, 123, 182, 184
Custer, Boston: 60, 67, 115, 122
Custer, Gen. G.A: 39, 74-76, 85-86, 97-99, 109-13, 117-19, 124-25, 129, 181-82, Black Hills Expedition of 1874, 24; discussion with Herendeen, 46-47, 173; leads 7th Cavalry in 1876 Sioux Expedition, 27; march from Ft. Lincoln, 29; consultation with Terry and Gibbon aboard *Far West*, 41; receives orders from Terry, 42-43; his march up the Rosebud, 44-49; discovers Indian trail leaves Rosebud, 46-47; marches up Davis Creek, 51; divides regiment into battalions, 56-59; begins his "reconnaissance in force," 61; arrives at Lone Tepee, 61; orders Reno to charge Indians, 62; turns north from Reno Creek, 64, 100, 176; arrives at Cedar Coulee, 65, 100; passes morass, 69; seen on bluffs by Reno's men, 71, 100, 177; reaches Medicine Tail Coulee, divides command, 102-03; ascends Luce Ridge, 104-05; seen by Indians, 104; rides to Nye-Cartwright Ridge, 107, 115; crosses to Calhoun Hill,

INDEX 189

116; reaches Custer Hill, 117; the Last Stand, 120-23; his strategy criticized, 131; his strategy defended, 132; cumulative causes of his defeat, 132-35
Custer, Lt. Col. Thomas W: 59, 103, 181, gives Kanipe message for McDougall, 64-65; body found on Custer Hill, 122

Dacotah Indians (Sioux): 20
Dakota, Military Dept. of: 26
Darcy, James W: 94
Darris, Pvt. John: 184
Davis Creek, Montana: 34, 36, 39, 49-51, 131
Dayton, Washington: 124
Deep Coulee: 114
Deep Ravine: 118-19
DeRudio, Lt. Charles: 58, 66, sees Custer on bluffs, 71, 177; with Sgt. White on skirmish line, 73, 177; supports Reno's decision to halt charge, 75; left behind in the timber, 78; rejoins Reno-Benteen on the bluffs, 95; gives opinion of timber position, 133; his reputation for veracity, 176; sees Benteen approaching Reno Hill, 179; locates body of Cpl. Foley, 183
DeWolf, Dr. James: 58, 80, 177
Dirty Moccasin, Cheyenne warrior: 31
Dorman, Isaiah: 30, 58, 77
Dose, Trumpeter Henry: 59, 121
Duggan, Pvt. John: 184

Edgerly, Lt. Winfield S: 57, recalls Custer's talk to officers on the Rosebud, 44-45; on number of hostiles believed assembled, 45; on examining Tulloch's Creek, 47-48; describes trail of the hostiles, 49; on Custer at Crow's Nest, 51; on hostiles' discovery of troops, 52; describes Benteen's orders, 57; describes Benteen's scout to the left, 67; on number of hostiles opposing Reno, 74; starts for Weir Point, 82-83; arrives at Weir Point, 84-85; retreats to Reno Hill, 87-88; describes soldiers on Reno Hill, 90; describes hostile attack on June 26, 92; estimates actual strength of hostiles, 130; his opinion of Custer's strategy, 132; sees wounded grey horse after battle, 184
Ellison, Douglas W: 124, 175

Far West steamer: 30, 32, 174
Fehler, Sgt. Henry: 93
Finckle, Sgt. August: 119
Finkel, Frank: 124, 175
Finley, Sgt. Jeremiah: 119
Fischer, Trumpeter Charles: 79
Fitzgerald, Farrier John: 175
Fitzpatrick, Thomas: 22
Foley, Cpl. John of Co. "C": 110-11, 113, 121, 180, 182-83
Foley, Pvt. John of Co. "K": 123, 180, 183
Foolish Elk, Ogallala warrior: 183
Forsyth, Gen: 29
Fort Abraham Lincoln, North Dakota: 27, 29, 45
Fort Custer, Montana: 182-83
Fort Ellis, Montana: 27, 29
Fort Fetterman, Wyoming: 27, 29, 33
Fort Laramie Treaties of 1851, 1868: 19, 22, 24
Fort Pierre, South Dakota: 21, 171
Fort Shaw, Montana: 27, 29
French, Capt. Thomas: 58, 77, describes Reno's retreat, 78; advances to Weir Point, 84; ordered back to Reno Hill, 86-87; on Reno Hill, 90

Gall, Uncpapa warrior: 112, 118-19
Garryowen, Montana: 56
Gatling guns: 29
Geiger, Sgt. George: 93
Gerard, Fred: 58, 61, 98, 134, reports Indians "running away," 61, 176; rides ahead with scouts, 63; reports to Cooke, 64; left behind in timber, 78; rejoins command on Reno Hill, 95; hears firing from Custer, 115; criticizes Reno's valley fight, 133
Gibbon, Gen. John: 27, 30, 32, 44, 48, 50, 58, 61, 122-23, 125, 131, march from Ft. Shaw to the Rosebud, 29; conference aboard *Far West*, 41-43; appraisal of Reno's timber position, 133
Gibson, Lt. Frank: 57, 67, 87, 90

190 THE CUSTER MYSTERY

Gilbert, Pvt. John M: 76, 93
Glenn, Pvt. George: 123, 126-27
Godfrey, Lt. Edward: 56, 68, 81, 108, 127, 133, 183, recalls Custer's talk to officers on Rosebud, 44-45; comments on examination of Tulloch's Creek, 47-48; comments on Terry's orders to Custer, 48-49; remarks on firing heard from Custer, 83; views Custer Battlefield from Weir Point, 86; on retreat from Weir Point, 87-88; comments on Custer's actions, 112; on finding cavalry horse on Rosebud, 124; on expected Indian strength, 130; on causes of defeat, 132-33
Goldin, Pvt. Theodore: 93, 131
Goose Creek, Wyoming: 27, 33, 39, 131
Graham, Lt. Col. William A: 131
Greenleaf Creek, Montana: 32
"Grey Horse" Troop (Co. "E"): 116-17, 182, 184
Grinnell, George B: 21, 114
Gros Ventre Indians: 22

Hagemann, Cpl. Otto: 183
Hale, Capt. Owen: 56
Hanging Woman Creek, Wyoming: 27
Hanley, Sgt. Richard: 124, 185
Hardin (MT) *Tribune:* 183
Hare, Lt. Luther: 57-58, 63, 83, 107-08, 133, 179, comments on Reno's valley fight, 75; sent for packtrain and returns, 82; at Weir Point, 86-88; comment on cause of defeat, 131
Harrington, Lt. Henry: 59, 119, 122
Harris, Pvt. David: 93
Hart, B.H. Liddell: 98
He Dog, Ogallala warrior: 110, 112, 114, 120
Helmer, Pvt. Julius: 89
Herendeen, George: 58, discussion with Custer on Rosebud, 46, 173; on enemy strength against Reno, 75; left behind in the timber, 78; hears firing from Custer, 115, 183-84; mentions Nathan Short, 127
Heyn, 1st Sgt. William: 72
Hidatsa Indians: 20
Hodgson, Lt. Benjamin: 58, 79, 83

Hohmeyer, 1st Sgt. Edward: 123
Hughes, Pvt. Francis: 123
Hughes, Sgt. Robert: 59, 123
Hunter, Pvt. Frank: 175

Illsley, Capt. Charles: 56
Indian Creek, Montana: 37-38
"Indian Paradise": 36

Jackson brothers: 30
Jackson, William: 95
James River, South Dakota: 171
Johnson, Pvt. Benjamin: 79

Kanipe, Sgt. Daniel: 60, 64, 69, 125, 127, 176
Kellogg, Mark H: 60, 122
Keogh, Lt. Col. Miles: 114, 121, 131, 133, given command of a battalion, 59, 103; ascends Luce Ridge, 104, 106; approaches Calhoun Hill from Nye Cartwright Ridge, 115; moves to Calhoun Hill position, 116; attacked by Crazy Horse, 119
King, Sgt. George: 89
Kiowa Indians: 21
Klotzbucher, Pvt. Henry: 76, 78
Korn, Blacksmith Gustave: 78
Kuhlman, Dr. Charles: 61, 108, 175

Lame White Man, Cheyenne warrior: 31, 117
Lake of the Woods, Minnesota: 21, 171
La Verendrye, Pierre: 20
Lee, Lt. Jesse: 109
Le Forge, Thomas H: 32, 101
Le Jeune, Paul: 20
Lewis and Clark Expedition: 21, 171
Little Big Horn Battle: 24, 109
Little Big Horn River: 34, 36, 39, 41, 43, 48-50, 55, 61-62, 64, 71, 104, 131, 135
Little Hawk, Cheyenne warrior: 34, 36
Little Missouri River, WY-ND: 21
Little Owl Creek, Montana: 36
Little Powder River, Montana: 27, 30
Little Wolf, Cheyenne warrior: 23
Lodge Pole Creek, Wyoming: 27
"Lone Tepee": 61-63, 69
Lord, Dr. George E: 59, 122

INDEX

Lorentz, Pvt. George: 78
Lounsberry, Col. C.A: 60
Lucca, Marion: 181
Luce, Major Edward S: 104, 106-07, 175, 179, 182
Luce Ridge: 104-07, 114, 115
Lynch, Pvt. Dennis: 122, 175

Madden, Pvt. Michael: 93-94
Mad Wolf, Cheyenne warrior: 114
Mandan Indians: 20
Mann, F.C: 91
Marquis, Dr. Thomas: 32, 56
Martin, Cpl. James: 78, 183
Martin, Trumpeter John: 60, 123, 176, leaves Custer battalions, 65, 100, 181; meets Boston Custer, 66; delivers message to Benteen, 69
Mathey, Lt. Edward: 59-60, 83, 122
McCormick, Pvt. Samuel: 78
McDougall, Capt. Thomas: 65, 82, 131, 133, assigned to guard packtrain, 59; personnel under his command, 60; march from Divide to morass, 67; reaches Reno Hill, 83; identifies Co. "E" bodies in ravine, 121, 123; meets Hare coming from Reno Hill, 179
McGonigle, Pvt. Hugh: 92
McGuire, Pvt. John: 127
McIlhargey, Pvt. Archibald: 60
McIntosh, Lt. Donald: 56, 58, 77
Mecklin, Blacksmith Henry: 93
Medicine Tail Coulee: 65-66, 101-08, 110, 112-14, 123, 175
Meier, Pvt. John H: 72
Merrill, Col. Lewis: 56
Miles, Gen. Nelson A: 136
Mills, Major Anson: 28, 38
Minneconjou Sioux Indians: 31
Minnesota: 20
Missouri, Military District of: 24, 26
Missouri River: 21-23, 171
Mitchell, D.D: 22
Mitchell, Pvt. John: 60
Mizpah Creek, Montana: 30
Montana: 24, 26-27, 33

Moore, Pvt. Andrew: 92
Morass: 67-69
Morris, Pvt. William: 177
Moylan, Capt. Myles: 58, 178

New Mexico: 22
New York *Herald:* 41, 87, 176-77
Nez Perce Indians: 25
Nye-Cartwright Ridge: 107-08, 114-16, 135
Nye, Col. Edward L: 107

Ogallala Sioux Indians: 22, 28-31, 110, 116-18, 171
O'Hara, Sgt. Miles: 72
Old Horn, Fred: 101
O'Neill, Pvt. Thomas: 71, 78, 95
Otter Creek, Montana: 27

Patten, Trumpeter John: 119
Pease Bottom, Montana: 124
Petring, Pvt. Henry: 71, 77, 79, 92, 122
Pierre, South Dakota: 171
Pigford, Pvt. Edward: 93
Platte, Military Dept. of: 24, 26
Plenty Coups, Crow chief: 21
Ponca Indians: 171
Porter, Dr. Henry R: 58, 74, 94
Porter, Lt. James: 59, 113, 122
Powder River, MT—WY: 27-31, 33, 129
Prairie Dog Creek, Wyoming: 33-34
Pretty Face, Arickara scout: 60
Pumpkin Creek, Montana: 30

Quinn, James: 125

Rafter, Sgt. John: 180
Rapid City *Journal:* 173
Raymier, Pvt: 125
Red Lake, Minnesota: 21, 171
Reed, Harry A: 60, 122
Reily, Lt. William Van W: 59, 122
Reno Creek: 36, 38, 55, 61-64, 67-68, 83
Reno Hill: 64-65, 80, 82-85, 87-88, 100, 108, 118, 123, 134
Reno, Col. Marcus: 43-44, 61, 69, 83-84, 86, 88, 104-07, 112-13, 122, 131, 133-35, 175,

179, reconnaissance from Powder River, 30; reports to Terry, 41; assigned battalion, 58, 60; ordered to charge Indians, 62, 175; on march down Reno Creek, 63-64; begins charge up valley, 71; forms skirmish line, 72; moves troops to the timber, 72-74; seen fighting by Bouyer and Curly, 66, 100-01; retreats to bluffs, 76-80, 181; joined on hill by Benteen, 81; sends Hare for packtrain, 82; at Weir Point, 85-87, 123; on Reno Hill, 88-92; his actions reviewed, 132-33
Reynolds, Charlie: 30, 47, 58, 64, 76
Reynolds, Col. John J: 27-29, 129
Robb, Pvt. Eldorado: 77
Rocky Mountains: 22
Roe, Lt. Charles: 125
Rosebud River, Montana: 29-30, 32-39, 41-47, 49-50, 55, 111, 124-27, 174
Rott, Sgt. Louis: 180
Roy, Sgt. Stanislas: 71, 76, 91-94, 110, 121
Royall, Col. William B: 33, 38
Rutten, Pvt. Roman: 72, 76-77, 79, 91, 94 127
Ryan, 1st Sgt. James: 77, 89-90, 94, 181

St. Louis, Missouri: 20
Sans Arcs Sioux Indians: 31
Santee Sioux Indians: 31
Scollin, Cpl. Henry: 77
Scott, Gen. Hugh: 176, 182
Sharrow, Sgt.-Major William H: 59
Sharpshooters Hill: 89
Sheridan, Col. Michael: 56
Sheridan, Lt. Gen. Phil: 24, 26, 29, 40, 48, 130, 174
Sheridan, Wyoming: 33
Sherman, General William T: 45
Short, Pvt. Nathan: 125-28
Shoshone Indian scouts: 33-34, 37
Sievertson, Pvt. John: 78
Sioux Creek, Montana: 32
Sioux Indians: 19, 28, 34, 114, 133, migration to Missouri River, 20-22, 171; at Ft. Laramie Treaty signing, 1851, 22; received western South Dakota as reservation, 23; at Ft. Laramie Treaty signing, 1868, 23-24; reservation boundaries redefined by Agreement of 1876, 25; attack Crook on the Rosebud, 37-38; move down Reno Creek to Little Big Horn, 55; horseherders see Reno's approach, 64; estimates of numbers opposing Reno, 74; pursue retreating soldiers to bluffs, 77; long distance firing at Custer battalions, 107; Gall and Crazy Horse destroy Keogh battalion, 119
Sitting Bull, Uncpapa medicine man: 130, 185
Smith, Capt. Algernon: 56, 59, 103, 122
Smith, Capt. E.W: 43
Smith, Pvt. George E: 72, 177
South Dakota: 171
Spotted Tail, Brule chief: 22
Standing Bear, Brule warrior: 111-12
Stands In Timber, John: 23
Stewart, Dr. Edgar I: 174, 183
Stoker, Pvt: 125
Sturgis, Lt. James: 59, 116-17, 119, 121-22
Sturgis, Gen. Samuel: 56
Sun River, Montana: 27, 29

Table of Equitation: 62, 175
Tall Bull, Cheyenne warrior: 109, 112, 121
Tanner, Pvt. James: 93-94, 180
Taylor, Blacksmith Walter O: 91
Terry, Gen Alfred H: 40, 44-51, 58, 61, 123, 130-31, appointed expedition commander, 26; on march from Ft. Lincoln, 29-30; at mouth of the Rosebud, 41; issues orders to Custer, 42-43; his report to Sheridan, 48
Teton Sioux Indians: 20
Texas: 22
Thompson, Pvt. Peter: 93, 175, 180
Thompson, Col. Richard E: 122, 127
Throssel, Mr: 183
Tilford, Lt. Col. Joseph: 56
Tongue River, Montana: 27, 30-31, 41, 43, 49
Tourtellotte, Col. John: 56
Tulloch's Creek, Montana: 43, 46-47, 173
Turley, Pvt. Henry: 72
Turtle Rib, Minneconjou warrior: 183
Tweed, Pvt. Tom: 123
Two Moons, Cheyenne warrior: 183

Uncpapa Sioux Indians: 31-32, 55, 71, 73, 110, 119, 175

INDEX

Varden, 1st Sgt. Frank: 119
Varnum, Lt. Charles: 51-52, 57-58, 84, 94, 178
Vickory, Sgt. John: 122
Voit, Saddler Otto: 93
Voss, Chief Trumpeter Henry: 59, 122

Wagoner, John C: 59
Wallace, Lt. George: 52, 58, keeps itinerary of march from Divide, 62-63; leaves timber during retreat, 76; on supposed ammunition shortage, 84; views Custer Battlefield from Weir Point, 86; establishes Co. "G" defensive line on Reno Hill, 89
War Department: 26, 45, 130
Washita, Battle of: 98, 132-33
Watson, Pvt. James: 175
Weir Point: 65, 83-86, 88, 100, 102, 104, 108, 118, 123, 177, 181
Weir, Lt. Col. Thomas: 44, 57, 68, 82-86, 108
White Bear, Russell: 123, 182
White, Sgt. Charles: 73, 78-79, 177
White River, South Dakota: 22, 171
White Shield, Cheyenne warrior: 114
Widmayer, Pvt. Ferdinand: 126
Wilber, Pvt. James: 93-94, 124

Windolph, Pvt. Charles: 93
Winney, 1st Sgt. DeWitt: 89
Wisconsin: 20
Wolf Mountains, Montana: 34, 36, 51
Wood Creek, Montana: 31
Wooden Leg, Cheyenne warrior: 99, 112, born in Black Hills, 21; at Powder River fight, 29; describes tribal movements, 30-32, 34; member of hunting party, 32, 34; in camp on Little Big Horn, 55-56; in Reno's valley fight, 73, 77-78; sees Custer's troops downstream, 105-07; describes action on Custer Battlefield, 113, 115-17, 119-20, 127-28
Wyoming: 22, 36

Yates, Lt. Col. George: 52, 111, 131, 133, given command of battalion, 59, 103; moves toward Medicine Tail Ford, 104, 114; moves to Calhoun Hill, 115; moves to Custer Hill, 116
Yates, George L: 174
Yellow Hair, Cheyenne warrior: 56
Yellowstone River, Montana: 26, 29-32, 36, 41, 43, 124-26, 130, 184

Designed by Robert Clark
Produced under the direction of the
Arthur H. Clark Co.
P.O. Box 14707
Spokane, WA 99214